Mark Gold

# Assault and battery

## What factory farming means for humans and animals

Pluto  Press

First published in 1983 by Pluto Press Limited,
The Works, 105a Torriano Avenue, London NW5 2RX
and Pluto Press Australia Limited, PO Box 199,
Leichhardt, New South Wales 2040, Australia.

Copyright © Mark Gold 1983

Set by Grassroots Typeset, London NW6
Printed and bound in Great Britain by
Garden City Press, Letchworth, Herts

British Library Cataloguing in Publication Data
Gold, Mark
 Assault and battery
 1. Animals, Treatment of – Great Britain
 2. Livestock – Great Britain
 I. Title
 636       HV4708

ISBN 0-86104-727-3

'Come, Marlow' I said, 'you exaggerate surely—if only by your way of putting things. It's too startling.'

'I exaggerate!' he defended himself. 'My way of putting things! My dear fellow I have merely stripped the rags of business verbiage and financial jargon off my statements. And you are startled! I am giving you the naked truth. It's true that nothing leaves itself open to the charge of exaggeration more than the language of naked truth.'

Joseph Conrad from Chance

# Contents

**Part three    Time for a change**

# Acknowledgements

It is impossible to give recognition to the many literary influences which helped to shape this book, but I am very conscious of the huge impression made by the late E.F. Schumacher with *Small is Beautiful*.

On a more personal note, I would like to thank Anna for starting me thinking about it all and everybody who has helped develop my interest, particularly Peter Roberts at Compassion in World Farming, from whom I have learnt so much about farming methods. Shelley, Geraldine, my sister Zoe, Lyn, Emily and Jean Pink, typed, read or reassured along the way and I am grateful to them all. John May has contributed many helpful criticisms and his advice has been invaluable in improving the text. I am also indebted to Clare, Penny and Matthew Evans, who gave me a home to work from and made me feel one of the family. Above all, thanks are due to Joy and the late Harry Coombes for their friendship, guidance, encouragement and immeasurable support over the years.

Finally, a word of appreciation for the active supporters of Compassion in World Farming: their dedication to the fight against factory farming has often revived flagging spirits.

# Introduction

More than 10 years ago now, a friend showed me some leaflets outlining how animals were treated on modern farms. I cannot remember the exact details of the literature, but I do recall still the first pictures I ever saw of veal calves solitarily confined in narrow crates and hens packed ruthlessly into battery cages. They came as quite a shock to someone who had spent the first 20 years of his life consuming vast quantities of animal produce at almost every meal, blissfully ignorant of the processes by which steaks and chicken breasts had arrived on his plate. Previously, I do not think I had given so much as a thought to the fact that meat was actually dead animal, let alone to methods of production.

I cannot claim that this first confrontation with factory farming prompted immediate action. After all, meat eating was such an enjoyable habit. How could I live without basing every meal around it? Had it not been for several reminders from the same friend and more literature and photographs, there is every possibility that I should have carried on regardless. But the more I read, the less I felt able to ignore. Slowly the conviction grew that apart from representing a potent example of the age-old story of people's inhumanity to animals, factory farming raised other important questions. The vast scale of exploitation made possible by advances in technology and the sheer cold efficiency of this new form of violence to other life forms, seemed to carry dangerous ramifications for mankind too. Was there a link between increasing violence in human society and the way we were treating animals? Why was technology being used to create new and more extreme abuses for other creatures, rather than as the means to reduce suffering? Suddenly, the fight against factory farming was not simply about 'loving' animals; it was a campaign to respect all life and to try and create conditions where such a respect may flourish.

For the past five years, I have enjoyed an almost unique opportunity to examine these issues in some depth. Having done so, I believe emphatically that factory farming is not only immeasurably cruel, but also economically unnecessary, wasteful, unhealthy and damaging to efforts to alleviate human hunger in the world. Furthermore, the defences put forward for it are at best, specious, and at worst, deliberately misleading in order to protect those who make a profit.

This book is not the work of an 'agricultural expert'. To those who would dismiss what I have to say on those grounds, I can only say that I believe the concept of 'specialists' possessing magic knowledge outside the understanding of lesser mortals has already been applied too readily, in too many areas of life, in order to confuse and distort what are essentially simple truths. Moreover, we can hardly expect balanced judgements from within the farming industry, since history demonstrates repeatedly that with a few notable exceptions, those with interests in any social evil are normally its most outspoken defenders.

What I have to say is not anti-farmer. Like any other group of humans, farmers are a mixture of good, bad and indifferent. The majority of them follow rather than set trends and it would be naive to blame the farming community for the spread of factory farming. The main impetus behind modern animal production has come from mammoth financial interests who have seen animal protein as an easy source of profits. Above all, it is they who are 'getting away with murder'.

The majority of battery farmers and slaughterhouse owners are less than enthusiastic about visits from declared opponents of their practices. For this reason, it has proved impossible to verify personally all accusations made in the text. Nevertheless, by fair means or foul, every effort has been made to observe at first hand the conditions described. Where this has not been feasible, information is based largely upon reports in farming journals, which are themselves revealing in the language they use.

Most of the figures quoted are taken either from the same sources or from official Ministry of Agriculture statistics. They are employed in full recognition of the fact that statistics can be twisted and distorted in order to prove more or less anything and are offered only as a useful guide to the size and complexity of the factory farming industry, not as a minutely accurate assessment. Ultimately, the suffering inflicted upon millions of individual farm animals cannot be quantified.

I hope that the reader who notices some illogicality in the subtitle of this book will bear with me. I am well aware that we humans are ourselves animals, not, as the subtitle might imply, a totally unrelated species. Nevertheless, the differentiation seemed necessary in order to impress upon the unconvinced reader that this book concerns an important human problem, and not simply cruelty to farm animals.

Mark Gold

# List of committees and reports

The following committees and reports are, at various times, referred to in the text.

**The Brambell Report**
Following the first exposé of factory farming in Ruth Harrison's book, *Animal Machines* (1964), the government set up a committee of investigation with Professor Brambell as chairperson. The ensuing report, although considered a compromise, did at least offer certain basic protection for animals. It has been largely ignored.

**The Farm Animal Welfare Advisory Committee (FAWAC)**
The government of the day set up FAWAC, following the Brambell Report, to advise on welfare matters. It existed for 13 years and its achievements can most generously be described as negligible.

**The Swann Report (1969)**
An attempt to curb the widespread and indiscriminate use of antibiotics in animal rearing.

**The Codes of Practice for the Rearing of Farm Animals (1971)**
These contain guidelines on the keeping of livestock, to which farmers are supposed to adhere, including space allowances per animal. Apart from the fact that they are hopelessly inadequate, they also lack the full force of law, being only voluntary.

**The Farm Animal Welfare Council (FAWC)**
In 1980 the Minister of Agriculture, Peter Walker, disbanded FAWAC and replaced it with FAWC. Although the latter has been granted more scope than its predecessor, its members again comprise an irreconcilable

mixture of those opposed to factory farming and those with vested interests in it. At present, the latter include a battery-hen farmer, a director from a firm involved in the live export trade, and the chief consultant veterinary surgeon from one of Britain's largest poultry interests.

## The Draft Revised Codes of Practice

Since its conception, FAWC has been concerned mainly with the production of draft proposals for revising the 1971 Codes of Practice. Papers produced show an overall improvement on the existing codes, without going anywhere near far enough to please those committed to the abolition of factory farming. The main problem is that they remain voluntary codes, rather than mandatory regulations enforceable by law. The first official revised codes — for pigs and cattle — were published in May 1983.

## The Ammedown Report 1980

The report of a seminar in which a group of 'experts' involved in the meat trade in one way or another, all voiced concern about the suffering endured by animals between farm and slaughterhouse.

## The House of Commons Select Committee on Agriculture, Report on Animal Welfare in Poultry, Pig and Veal Calf Production

A group of MPs investigated factory farming and caused considerable controversy when their report was published in 1981. They condemned both factory farming of pigs and veal calves and recommended a five-year run-down programme leading to a permanent ban on battery cages for hens. All their suggestions were rejected by the government.

## EEC Draft Directive for the Protection of Laying Hens (1982)

Two years of debate in the EEC ended with this directive recommending that all battery hens in the EEC should be allowed $500cm^2$ after 1990. This proposal represents a hopeless compromise on what was originally an investigation to seek alternatives to the cage. Moreover, some EEC countries refuse even this minute advancement. Further compromise is likely — probably reducing the space allowance to $450cm^2$ per bird.

Part one

# Tales from the farmyard...

# 1. Poultry

## Battery eggs

Even before the second world war a few farmers kept small flocks of egg-laying chickens in single-bird battery cages, though the practice was not common. It was after the war that numbers increased steadily and in the 1950s and early 1960s the egg industry began to develop into the multimillion pound concern it is today. By 1961, 19 per cent of the UK's total egg output derived from battery cages;[1] a figure that has now risen to over 96 per cent.[2] Multinational companies infiltrated the market, bringing high-powered advertising and aggressive sales techniques. The scale of operation increased dramatically. Small farmers were taken over by big concerns or produced eggs on contract to them; average flock size multiplied from hundreds to thousands and then to tens of thousands; batteries replaced deep-litter, which had itself taken over from free-range as the standard method of production. (Ministry of Agriculture figures show that in 1960/61, 49.8 per cent of eggs came from deep-litter systems,[3] with a further 30 per cent on free-range. In 1981/82 these numbers had diminished to 1.9 per cent and 1.7 per cent respectively.) Also, single-bird cages were replaced by cages carrying two, three and eventually four, five or even six or more birds.

Over the decades, poultry geneticists, employed by large-scale commercial enterprises, have bred birds which they claim are perfectly suited to battery cages. Never satisfied, however, vested interests continue to sponsor widespread research in search of an even more productive model. Apart from docility to counteract the strain and aggression associated with close confinement, the qualities sought are increased productivity as far as egg laying is concerned, and increased economy in the bird's capacity to lay more eggs in return for less food. On average, battery birds now lay approximately 250 eggs each a year, compared to 199 on free-range and 226 on deep-litter.[4]

There are three popular strains of bird: white hens for white eggs, brown hens for brown and a lighter coloured hen for what are sometimes called tinted eggs. It is a measure of the egg industry's successful advertising that many people still believe that brown eggs are a sign of healthy outdoor birds. This is total myth. Shell colour depends entirely upon the breed of hen.

Breeding stock are usually kept in large sheds on a deep-litter system. Light, heat and feed are carefully controlled. Once a week the eggs are transferred to hatcheries. Hatching takes approximately three weeks, after which the sex of the day-old chicks is determined by 'highly skilled' operators.[5] Females, known henceforth as pullets, are then vaccinated and packed and loaded onto purpose-built lorries, ready to begin commercial life. Male chicks are not treated so carefully. Since they cannot lay eggs and are not genetically bred to fatten up quickly for human consumption, they are considered economically useless. Consequently, they are 'humanely destroyed'. There are no laws governing euthanasia of day-old chicks, so a variety of methods exist. Some are 'homogenized' (i.e. crushed) by a special mill capable of mincing 1,000 chicks to pulp every two minutes. The resulting 'mush' can be used for either animal feed or manure. Other popular methods include decompression through oxygen withdrawal, and gassing with chloroform or more popularly carbon dioxide, for which simple gas chambers have been developed.

From the poultry industry's point of view these methods have one drawback. Crushers and gas chambers cost money to install and there are no profits in return for investment. Often, therefore, they resort to suffocation, which is cheaper. Thousands of chicks are packed on top of each other and tied together in sacks or solid containers. In the resulting struggle for air, some chicks are squashed to death, some suffocate quickly and the strongest, having won the fight to the top, die more slowly. Suffocation through drowning is another method sometimes applied.[6]

The national egg-laying flock fluctuates between 40 million and 60 million birds.[7] This means that roughly the same number of male chicks are 'humanely destroyed' at one day old, every year.

Pullets do not begin laying eggs for commercial production until they reach about 20 weeks. Until then, most live in long, windowless buildings where they are able to wander on a floor of wood shavings. Light is restricted and temperature is kept high. Rapidly gaining in popularity, however, is the concept of 'single stage' cage rearing, where pullets are kept in battery cages from a day old.[8]

By the time they reach 20 weeks, some 96 per cent of the nation's egg-laying flock are in battery cages, where they will stay for the rest of their lives. Present day stocking densities in this country allow four birds to a cage measuring 16 inches by 18 inches, or five birds to a cage 18 inches by 20 inches; in other words, 4 inches of cage width each. Since average wing span is about 30 inches, hens cannot spread one wing, let alone two. Yet when questioned on this point, the Ministry of Agriculture argue that freedom of movement is not totally prohibited.

> They often exercise their wings by stretching one leg and the wing on the same side of the body at the same time in a backwards direction. This movement requires considerably less space than wing flapping.[9]

Endless debate, argument and setting up of committees in the EEC has resulted in proposals for improved standards. But progress is painfully slow and developments are uninspired. Few of the EEC nations can reach agreement and what was originally an investigation into finding alternatives to battery production has fizzled out into a squabble over the number of centimetres to be allowed each battery bird. Furthermore, even the proposed space allowance per bird has been gradually whittled down, until the most likely outcome is that every battery bird in the EEC will be permitted 450cm after 1984, with further discussion postponed until the following year.[10] It is impossible to feel much enthusiasm for these measures when we realize that current codes of practice in the UK already allow 460cm per bird! Rather, it is evident that the EEC is being used primarily as a vehicle for postponing action from individual states.

Cages are usually stacked up to three or four tiers high in windowless buildings. Light intensity is maintained for up to 17 hours per day and temperature is kept constantly high. It is the combined effects of breeding, high-protein food, light and warmth that ensures high rates of egg production.

Both size and degree of automation vary considerably, but it is not unusual to find more than 20,000 birds in one shed, with light, heat, food, egg collection and dung removal all mechanized. Units are constantly increasing in size, particularly those owned by multi-national interests. Managing director of Daylay Eggs, a subsidiary of Britain's largest poultry concern, recently advocated 'an overall size unit of 80,000 birds split among two or three houses' for optimum production.[11]

The floors of battery cages are made of wire which allows dung to fall through onto a droppings belt beneath. The wire floor also slopes towards the front to allow eggs to roll onto another belt in front of the cage. Gripping a sloping wire floor often causes sore or deformed feet amongst birds.

Overcrowding promotes 'vices' such as feather pecking and canni-balism. Some hens are aggressive by nature, but this is seldom a serious problem when victims are able to take evasive action. Hens enjoy a strict pecking order and on less intensive systems  those at the bottom of the order usually keep out of the way of dominant birds. Where there are problems with pecking order in battery cages there is no possibility of escape. Despite attempts by geneticists to breed aggression out of battery stock, some producers still debeak birds routinely as a preventive measure. Figures are difficult to establish, though in a letter dated December 1982, the Ministry of Agriculture did not dispute that the number of birds debeaked was around 40 per cent.[12] The National Farmers' Union argue that 'not more than 10 per cent' of birds are operated upon. The Brambell Report (para. 97), recommending a ban, described the mutilation as follows:

> The upper mandible of the bird consists of a thin layer of horn covering a bony structure of the same profile which ex-tends to within a millimetre or so of the tip of the beak. Bet-ween the horn and the bone is a thin layer of highly sen-sitive soft tissue, resembling the quick of the human nail. The hot knife blade used in debeaking cuts through this com-plex of horn, bone and sensitive tissue causing severe pain.

Generally, the quality of battery eggs is inferior to those produc-ed by free-range methods. A Ministry of Agriculture letter, dated 19 May 1978, states:

With regard to the vitamin content of battery eggs, a detailed study of the nutritional value of eggs conducted by this ministry, found that, on average, battery hens produced eggs with 40 per cent less vitamin B12 and 30 per cent less folic acid than free-range eggs.[13]

Furthermore, in spite of routine use of antibiotics in poultry feed, the battery egg industry is still frequently struck by waves of 'baffling' infection. One of the most persistent diseases is 'seaside syndrome' or 'watery whites'. This causes egg whites, when the egg is broken, to run all over the pan instead of remaining in a tight, firm circle around the yolk. Some government officials believe it may be a result of infectious bronchitis in battery units.[14]

Many other health problems exist, specifically related to the barren environment of battery units. Fear and hysteria syndrome 'seems to increase with crowding' and is 'much more frequent on wire floors as compared to deep-litter pens'.[15] All battery hens suffer from pre-laying frustration because they are unable to lay their eggs in nests; the inability to exercise their wings 'reduces the strength of the wing bones and may result in broken wings' and also causes a general bone weakness that may eventually develop into a clinical disease known as 'cage layer fatigue'. The symptoms include lameness and stopping of laying and, as its name suggests, the disease is exclusive to cages. Another common degenerative condition is known as 'fatty liver syndrome'. Scientists are unsure of the exact cause, though a mixture of factors existing in batteries have been cited — amongst them, lack of exercise, stress, high temperature and overconsumption of food. The disease can prove fatal due to haemorrhage from the enlarged liver.

Such problems rarely reach the public ear. On the contrary, vast sums of money are invested in advertising to make eggs appear as attractive as possible. For 1983, the proposed figure for generic advertising alone was £3 million.[16] Every few months a new slogan is invented, nearly always associating eggs with green and pleasant pastures and country freshness. It is surely revealing that those who gain most from it are prepared to go to such extremes in order to perpetuate this myth.

Recent advertising emphasis has also been given to the golden-coloured yolk of battery eggs. Until a few years ago, this would have been a difficult campaign to undertake since battery yolks tended to be an unattractive pale colour. Nowadays, this is not a problem because it is permissible to add colouring agents to poultry feed in an attempt to produce golden-coloured yolks. Some substances used, like citranaxanthine, are amongst additives banned from food eaten directly by humans.[17]

Like almost all farm animals, battery hens are sent to death at an early age. For many years, standard practice was to send them to the slaughterhouse at the end of one period of laying, at approximately 15 months. Nowadays, the practice of keeping birds for a second year is increasingly popular. Second period egg-production is often 'aided' by the process of force-moulting. By causing birds severe shock, usually through food and water deprivation or a sharp contrast to the normal light pattern, it is possible to hurry birds through their moulting period (during which they do not lay eggs). Although hens do not lay quite as many eggs during the second year, those that they do lay tend to be larger and therefore command a higher price. In either case the end is the same.

At the end of either one or two periods of egg laying, hens are no longer considered economically viable. In the words of one producer, they are 'second-hand'. Despite the fact that 'second-hand' birds have many years of good egg laying left, they no longer keep up with the optimum performance levels demanded by the egg industry. By this time many hens are a wretched sight. A combination of raw necks, deformed feet, tattered feathers, pale combs, and abscesses and sores are frequently found.

## Broiler chickens

Although records suggest that the concept of keeping hens in cages for egg laying pre-dates the rearing of chickens for eating in broiler sheds, it was the latter that became the first widespread method of factory farming. Already by 1955, some 52 million birds were reared intensively and numbers have continued to increase. By 1963, 142 million chickens were kept under what we know as broiler conditions.[18] By 1981, that figure has reached 382 million,[19] resulting in more than 7 million birds being slaughtered every week in the UK alone.

In principle, both the selection of breeding stock and the hatching process are similar to battery egg production. But there are differences in the type of stock required for commercial broiler firms. Although docility to counteract aggression and stress is once again an important factor, the main quality sought is remarkable weight gain without much food consumption, thus allowing birds to be slaughtered as early as possible in return for the least investment.

Profit margins in broiler production have become increasingly tight over the years, forcing geneticists to search for novel ways of reducing production costs. Their latest innovation is a specially bred dwarf female bird called the mini-mother which has been introduced amongst breeding stock (i.e. the mothers of chickens fattened for eating). To the poultry industry this triumph of genetic breeding has two distinct virtues. Firstly, the mini-mother needs less food than normal-sized birds, and secondly she needs less room. Since breeding stock are not being fattened for eating, it pays particularly well to reduce the food bill and minimize space allowances. Normally, broiler breeding units hold about 8,000 birds. Using dwarf females, 9,600 can be placed in the same area.[20] In future, dwarf females are likely to be kept in battery cages, three to a standard five-bird cage. Progeny do not develop the dwarfing character.

One achievement that broiler geneticists share with their colleagues in the egg industry is that decades of extensive research have managed to create a whole range of disease problems. No sooner does routine use of antibiotics and vaccinations against known poultry diseases destroy one problem, than another rears its head. A member of the Ministry of Agriculture's own central veterinary laboratory has drawn attention to leg weaknesses said to affect 6 per cent of broiler stock − 22 million birds − a year. Other common injuries and diseases include marked disposition towards bone fractures and dislocations; leg and back injuries; a high incidence of heart attacks caused mainly by feeding high-energy diets to creatures whose bodies are not sufficiently developed; a miscellany of infectious diseases, liver problems and bacterial diseases such as arthritis and bumble foot.[21] A new infection now spreading through the nation's flock is known as 'runting syndrome'. Infected birds fail to develop properly and at four weeks old they are only half the normal weight and still covered in chick down. Sores in the pancreas and weak legs sticking out at angles are other symptoms.[22] Officials are forced to admit that the cause is unknown, though they maintain that there is no connection between 'runting syndrome' and dwarf female breeding stock.

This list by no means exhausts the tale of ill-health amongst broilers. Every morning, workers walk around the unit removing all the dead and dying birds. Even though the entire lifespan of broiler chickens is now only about 52 days,[23] mortality rates of 6 per cent are considered acceptable.[24] In other words, every year more than 20 million birds die before they reach 7 weeks old.

Commercial production methods begin when day-old chicks are transferred from the hatchery to the farm and placed in part of the broiler shed. Some are debeaked. For the first two weeks bright lights are employed to encourage feeding. Food and water are freely available from hoppers and troughs. At the end of that period, light intensity is usually reduced because of the danger that bright light may stimulate aggression. Partitions are removed from the shed and birds are allowed to move over the full area of the broiler shed.

At this early stage, the only possible source of criticism is the sheer number of birds reared in one shed, allowing no possibility of individual attention. This apart, there is little to complain about. In many ways living conditions are not unpleasant. Although windows are blacked out, light and ventilation is adequate, as is temperature. The floor is clean and covered with litter and food and water is plentiful and easily accessible.

It is when the chickens are nearly at slaughter weight, only five or six weeks later, that conditions become crowded. Birds fatten quickly on a high-protein diet, reaching an average slaughter weight of 3-4.5 lbs and by the time they approach this stage, the broilerhouse floor is one dense mass of chickens without any possibility of movement. Existing codes of practice recommend a minimum of $0.5ft^2$ per bird.[25] There is evidence that some farmers stock even more densely.

By this time, the floor is filthy with droppings; so much so that the smell (of ammonia) is overpowering to the visiting stranger. Lighting is dimmed further and many birds are unable to find their way to the food trough without climbing over others.

## Turkeys

Recently, turkey production has become the largest 'growth industry' amongst meat products. In the last 20 years, the number of birds slaughtered each year has risen from 3 million to more than 23 million.[26] In that time, turkey has changed from a luxury to a convenience food. Nowadays, it is available not only as an 'oven ready' product, but also cut up and processed into a whole range of supermarket packages.

Methods of production are similar to those employed with broiler chickens. On the most modern units, approximately 20,000 birds are reared in one building, partitioned into four groups of 5,000. Food and water are provided on an *ad lib* basis.

Relatively speaking, overcrowding is not as bad as in broiler chickenhouses, although producers do stock slightly above the levels recommended by the Brambell Committee. Brambell recommended 1.5ft² at 8-12 weeks, and 4ft² above 12 weeks. Britain's largest producers allow a minimum of 1.25ft² up to 8 weeks, 2.5ft² up to 16 weeks, and 3.5ft² over 16 weeks.[27]

Fed a high-protein diet, based on grain and soya, turkeys put on weight quickly. Unlike broiler chicken units, where the shed is usually cleared in one swoop, turkeys are taken at different weights. Some birds are transported for slaughter at 13 weeks, 12lb turkeys at about 15 weeks, and bigger birds at 18 weeks. By this time, all female birds, which produce meat for the oven-ready market, have been slaughtered. But males are reared on up to 24 weeks for further processed foods like turkey ham or turkey sausages. It has been discovered that with added colouring and flavouring, turkey will take the taste of almost any meat. As it is also cheaper to produce per pound than (say) pork or beef, this has led to this new range of processed turkey foods appearing on the market.

Despite 'hygienic conditions' and liberal availability of food and water, some turkeys grow bedraggled and deformed. Mortality rates stand at about 5 per cent, heart attacks being the main cause of death.

## Poultry transportation

When birds leave battery cages or broiler sheds at the end of their 'commercial life', they are treated with so little regard for their individual welfare that widespread suffering between farm and 'processing plant' — as chicken slaughter houses are termed — is ensured.

Let us examine the fate of broiler chickens first. The process of transportation begins with the arrival of catching teams, often in the dark hours to minimize panic amongst the birds. A group of birds are fenced off in one part of the shed and the catching teams normally divide themselves into a chain-gang between the birds and the transportation vehicle. (On the latest transporters, batches of crates, moveable by forklift trucks, are actually brought into the sheds so that the chickens can be packed indoors). Chickens are grabbed by the legs and passed down the line until they are shoved into crates. A full load usually carries something in the region of 7,000 birds (obviously there is some variation according to size of both lorries and birds), packed tightly, into small crates 3ft by 2ft by 1ft. Several welfare problems present themselves even before the lorries leave for the slaughterhouse. For one thing, the chickens are frightened. Hitherto, their whole existence has taken place in fully environmentally controlled buildings. Now, they are suddenly tossed about from person to person, during whatever weather conditions happen to prevail. In addition, handling is often rough. Faced with the prospect of clearing shed after shed, each packed with 20,000 or more squawking chickens, night after night, is not an occupation likely to promote sensitivity. Combined with the fact that broiler chickens are particularly prone to bone weaknesses, the sort of problems that arise are not difficult to imagine: a number of birds have their wings and legs dislocated or broken.

Some poultry transporters offer no protection from the weather whatsoever, unless the driver ties down a canopy in rough conditions. If he does this with a very full load there is a danger of suffocation for some chickens. In some cases, those packed on the outside may be freezing cold, whilst at the same time, there is lack of adequate ventilation in the centre.

The more modern poultry vehicles do, at least, offer summary protection against both the elements and the problems of lack of ventilation. Nevertheless, they do not overcome the basic difficulty. Firstly, considerable suffering is inevitable when creatures accustomed only to the confined world of broiler sheds are transported into the noisy, 'natural' world, in temperatures which may range from a mid-summer heatwave to a January blizzard. Such a transfromation demands extraordinary sensitivity in handling (and preferably controlled-environment lorries!); instead, all the chickens are likely to experience is rough handling, uncomfortable crates and jolting lorries. In addition, overcrowding also causes considerable stress. When criticized over offensively high stocking densities, the poultry industry's usual defence is that overcrowding is practised to prevent birds suffering injuries through being thrown about!

Certainly, being thrown about is one problem that does not occur during transportation. Sometimes lids or flaps are shut with wings or legs trapped, and occasionally a bird gets its head caught in the crate above and is hung. Moreover, if crates get damaged (as happens frequently with constant use) or flaps and lids are not closed down properly, then some birds will be sent hurtling from lorries, usually to a premature death splattered on tarmac. For battery hens, the method of transportation is much the same, though if anything, suffering is more intense. To begin with, bruises and injuries due to rough handling are likely to be greater when removing birds from cages than when they are kept on the open floor. Sometimes, after a year or so in a battery cage the chicken's feet actually grow fixed around the wire.

After they leave the battery unit 'spent hens' are, as a rule, transported greater distances than broilers. This is because 'processing plants' with the specific purpose of turning ex-battery birds into soups, pies, pastes, and other convenience foods, tend to be scattered around the country. Advertisements from such companies abound in the poultry press, some offering to collect birds from 'anywhere in the UK'[28] in order to meet demand. Consequently, battery hens may be driven from one end of the country to the other, crammed into crates like bits of rag, with limbs and feathers protruding out of the sides of lorries.

Essentially, poultry have no legal protection during transportation. The main legislation governing their welfare is the Conveyance of Live Poultry Order (1919); passed when there was no poultry industry to speak of and very few lorries. It is hopelessly inadequate. Presumably it was introduced chiefly to protect the transportation of a relatively small amount of poultry to markets. Obviously, the idea of moving around almost 450 million birds every year to highly mechanized slaughterhouses, purpose-built for mass disposal of poultry, could hardly have been dreamt about.

The 1919 order makes it an offence to keep animals on lorries 'longer than is reasonably necessary'. This wording can be, and is, made to mean almost anything. There is no time limit either to the length of journeys or to the period that birds can be left on lorries before slaughter. Indeed, relatively speaking, the agony of some hens may only be beginning when they arrive at the slaughterhouse. If the vehicle turns up at the plant after the staff have gone home, or during a particularly busy period, then the load will probably be left out all night. At best only a token effort at feeding and watering is possible, because how can one adequately feed thousands of chickens closely packed in crates? A water-hose and a bucket of grain tossed carelessly over the top is the only method available. In some cases, leaving birds overnight can prove catastrophic. For instance, in January 1982, at Shippams' chicken paste factory in Crediton, Devon, 'possibly thousands of birds', were discovered dead on a Monday morning after being transported from Cornwall the previous day and left overnight at the factory during freezing cold weather. Although death on such a large scale is comparatively rare, it is evident that to fit in with work schedules, lorry loads of birds are frequently left out all night, causing enormous misery and a significant number of deaths.

## Poultry slaughter

Death for poultry is consistent with the rest of their existence — degrading and sordid. Firstly, the same rough handling which characterizes their exit from the broiler, turkey or battery unit is likely to occur again when birds are taken out of crates for slaughter. More bruising and torn-off limbs may result. Indeed, handling at this stage is likely to be even worse, because unloaders are faced with an additional problem of attempting to keep a constant supply of birds on the often fast moving slaughter line. Although an Environmental Health Officer or District Veterinary Surgeon is supposed officially to inspect birds for disease and welfare reasons before slaughter, they often find themselves under such pressure with post-mortem inspection that only a minimal length of time during the day is spent examining the pre-slaughter process.

After unloading, the birds — already 'half stunned' by their journey, according to some officials — are hung upside down by their legs on a shackle line and taken on a conveyor belt system to their deaths. In the case of chickens, they must not be suspended upside down for more than three minutes before being rendered insensitive to pain; turkeys can be left for up to six minutes.[29]

Eventually, the birds reach the stunning apparatus. By far the most common method is a water-bath charged with a low level electric current. After their heads have been immersed in the bath, the poultry pass on to the throat slitter, anything between 10 seconds and 30 seconds later. Sometimes killing (by cutting the jugular vein) is practised manually, but more often on larger units an automatic knife is employed, usually followed by a back-up man, whose job it is to ensure the death of those birds missed by the first knife.

In practice, things may go wrong at all stages. An almost completely automatic system has one insurmountable limitation: not *all* chickens can be produced to a standard size or condition in order to fit in neatly with mechanization. Slight differences in size or minimal movement by the birds at crucial moments, can affect catastrophically the efficiency of equipment. There is widespread concern that many birds are not stunned properly. A report from the Farm Animal Welfare Council, undertaken at the specific request of the Minister of Agrigulture, reached the following conclusion:

> We believe it to be too readily assumed that poultry are properly stunned after passing through the electrical water-bath stunner. Superficially, the birds may indeed, appear to have been stunned but we consider that a substantial number may still be sensitive to pain.[30]

The voltage in the water-bath is kept deliberately low at between 70 volts and 90 volts, because producers do not want birds to die from electrocution before their throats have been cut. Although turning up the electricity to ensure death instantaneously would be more humane to the poultry, it would not be acceptable to commercial interests, who argue that birds do not 'bleed out' properly if they die before their throats have been slit. Consequently, they may be shocked sufficiently to immobilize them, but still be sensitive to pain. In addition, mistakes are caused by sheer indifference or ignorance about the technology on the part of the operators. Failure to adjust the level of the water-bath to the size of new consignments of birds is a common fault. As a result of this combination of factors, some birds reach the slaughter knife fully or partly conscious.

Alternatively, it may be at the killing point that the process goes wrong. Advertisements proclaim proudly that automatic killers are between 94 per cent and 96 per cent efficient, given optimum conditions. Even if optimum conditions ever exist in processing plants — which is doubtful — such a figure is unsatisfactory in relation to humane slaughter of living creatures. Depending upon how the revolving 'worm' — which is supposed to guide the neck to the correct position to meet the blade — is set, it is possible that, for example, those birds with short necks are not cut at all, whereas those with long straggly necks may be cut across the skull. Since the back-up man usually stands close to the automatic knife, there is a possibility that he will see blood oozing from a cut on the top of the head and assume that the system has worked efficiently. Moreover, with the slaughter line normally killing in excess of 1,000 birds an hour, it is difficult for the back-up killer to keep up, particularly when he has been on the shift for some time and concentration inevitably lapses. Obviously this problem also exists where there is no automatic knife and the whole operation is performed manually.

The possible consequences of these numerous loop-holes is summarized in the Farm Animal Welfare Council's report:

> When the cut is not properly made and satisfactory bleeding fails to take place, some birds will enter the scald tank before they are dead and some may show obvious signs of consciousness.[31]

Whilst affecting only a small minority of birds, all of the 'accidents' described so far are, to varying degrees, every-day occurrences. A small minority of almost 450 million birds slaughtered annually still adds up to an enormous number. The Ministry of Agriculture's argument that injuries 'need to be set in perspective against the total size of operations carried out'[32] is not good enough. It accepts that the grotesque size of operations prohibits any possibility of 'humane slaughter' for every living creature, whereas constructive action could at least reduce the staggering scale of operation amongst poultry processors.

Currently, Britain's largest turkey slaughterhouse, owned by Bernard Matthews Ltd., has the capacity to kill 90,000 birds per week; Buxted Chicken Ltd., process 74,000 broilers per day at their plant in the Wiltshire village of Sutton Benger.

Summarizing the animal welfare standards of the whole industry, the Farm Animal Welfare Council has this to say:

> The view is widely held that the nature of the slaughterhouse operations, their high degree of mechanization and their speed and scale, result in sentient creatures being treated with indiference. We have much sympathy with such views.[33]

FAWC made several recommendations for improvements. One of the least controversial was that the journey between loading and slaughter should be limited to 12 hours. Typically the poultry industry responded with a claim that 24 hours would be the shortest time-limit it could afford.[34] Meanwhile, the transport of millions of birds continues to be controlled by an order of 1919, with slaughter conditions governed by laws which have proved equally inadequate.

# 2. Pigs and cattle

## Pigs

Unlike poultry, now almost exclusively factory farmed, pigs are still kept under a variety of systems, some even allowing animals fresh air and freedom of movement. Nevertheless, all the trends described for intensive poultry production have now established themselves in pig farming, particularly the trend to bigger units and greater density. By 1980, 58.6 per cent of all pig herds in the UK had more than 100 sows, compared to less than 43 per cent in 1975.[1] Even herds of more than 300 are no longer uncommon. By comparison, in 1960, more than half our pig farmers had breeding herds of less than 20 sows.[2]

Both breeding and fattening stock (the latter reared for bacon, pork and ham) have been affected by these changes. Let us look first at the former. Ministry of Agriculture figures reveal that in 1981 there were more than 838,000 sows kept for breeding purposes. According to the lowest estimates 'a little more than half'[3] of these sows exist in close confinement systems; others estimates put the figure at somewhere around 60-70 per cent. Because of both their high level of intelligence and the long periods during which they endure intensive conditions, many believe that pigs represent the most unfortunate of all farm animals. The factory farm system works something like the following.

As soon as a sow comes into season she is 'served' by one, or maybe more than one, boar. Although popular in Europe, artificial insemination has yet to win the approval of Britain's pig farmers, with only an estimated 3½ per cent of births attributable to a.i.[4] Sometimes pigs are actually allowed outside for mating because some display a marked reluctance to 'perform' when imprisoned. For others, even copulation takes place in semi or full confinement. On some farms what are graphically described as 'rape racks' are employed.

After mating, natural behaviour is strictly inhibited. Sows are returned to individual stalls, where they remain throughout their 16½ week pregnancy. Although stall designs vary, the principle is always the same: denying exercise, movement, companionship, fresh air and often adequate light. Sometimes sows are tied by neck tethers fixed to the side of the crate; others are fastened by girdles, strapped around the midriff and then attached to the ground. In these two systems the back part of the stall is open, whereas in the third popular type there is a back gate or wall, but no tethers. Under all three systems, the pigs are able to stand up, lie down, drink water, and for approximately 20 minutes each day they enjoy the added privilege of feeding upon a diet of specially pelleted food.

Yet even these little luxuries are not always enjoyed without a price. For bigger sows, lying down comfortably may not be too easy. Although the 1971 welfare codes of practice state that 'sows and gilts... should be able to lie down normally', the Ministry of Agriculture recommends that the width of crates should be only 1.97-2.13 feet.[5] 'Normally' is a deliberately imprecise word and it is evident that large sows are unable to lie down in a crate only 2ft wide without their legs sticking out under the metal stall rails into the territory of the next pig.

Inadequate stall size is not the worst of a host of welfare problems. Where tethers are employed, sores and abrasions are often caused by their rubbing against the skin. One experienced pig farmer puts it like this:

> I have worked with tether systems in the past and I would not use them again. I have seen sows' necks become so raw because of the tether constantly rubbing that the collar has actually embedded in the animal's neck.[6]

Floor surfaces are an even bigger cause for concern. At present, the standard floor is dry concrete, often slatted at the back to allow dung and urine clearance. If the slats are not wider than the hoof itself, then the obvious discomfort of standing on them may eventually cause foot and leg disorders. Sometimes slats are not installed far enough up the length of the stall and so sows end up lying in their own muck.

By nature, pigs are scrupulously clean, their reputation for dirtiness belonging solely to their habit of wallowing in mud to lose heat. Many farmers will testify how much pigs loathe lying in their own excreta. Yet in dry-sow stalls (where the pigs are kept during pregnancy) they are often covered in patches of dung.

Other problems exist, including spinal disorders caused by pigs trying to bring their back legs forward off the slats and thereby putting pressure on the spine instead of the leg muscles.

Nowadays, completely solid floors are sometimes used to replace slats. Yet these only create other problems. The floors 'step downwards' at the back to assist drainage, and if the step begins too near the front of the stall, they may cut into the belly of bigger sows.[7]

Basically, the insurmountable difficulty is that however ingenious equipment designers have become, geneticists have not yet matched them with pigs similarly standardized in size. In the quantified world of factory farming, slight differences can result in considerable extra sufferering.

Defenders of dry-sow stalls admit one or two teething management problems with design, but argue that the basic principle is sound. On the other hand, critics are adamant that boredom, discomfort and prohibition of exercise combine to promote extreme frustration. The most obvious manifestation of this is the way that sows often gnaw at the iron frame in front of their crates. Given the opportunity, pigs will spend considerable periods rooting in the ground, but since there is no outlet for such instincts in a stall, the urge is redirected towards the only available object — a metal bar.

Advocates of confinement systems also claim that they are necessary to prevent fighting amongst sows. Some sows are aggressive and now that breeding units have reached such mammoth proportions, stockworkers are less likely to spot problems of bullying. Therefore, confinement stalls are defended on the grounds that they allow proper inspection and prevent fights. Two points emerge from this argument. If it is true, it should be taken as proof that large intensive units are unacceptable, not that continuous imprisonment is justified. Secondly, it leads one to wonder how roughly 40 per cent of pig farmers survive without resorting to factory farming, particularly when some of them also manage large numbers of pigs.

Some vets believe that many sows kept in stalls are frequently cold lying on concrete, and also hungry.[8] Although genetic breeding has produced exceptionally lean pigs in order to meet the demand for fatless meat, animals kept constantly pregnant and denied exercise, not surprisingly, tend to put on excess weight. So they are fed a regulated diet which may leave them feeling hungry, even though it satisfies minimal nutritional requirements. Conveniently, this diet also keeps costs down.

A few days before they are due to give birth, sows are transferred to farrowing quarters, where they are similarly confined in crates. Designs vary. Some do allow straw bedding, but far too many have solid concrete, or worse still, perforated metal floors.

Farrowing crates are employed because over the years human interference with pig breeding has resulted in many modern breeds producing clumsy mothers, liable to crush piglets. In most farrowing crates, piglets have a heated area, known as a 'creep', beside the crate, enabling them to reach across to the sow's teats without danger of being crushed.

Nevertheless, farrowing stalls remain a controversial subject, not only because they restrict the sow's movement during and after birth, but also because they inhibit her nesting instincts. Shortly before they are due to farrow, unrestricted sows will collect nesting material in order to build enormous nests. In crates, pigs are unable to fulfil this instinct. As a result one may see sows lapsing into stereotyped behaviour, pathetically and fruitlessly enacting nest-building behaviour with their legs and snout in their confinement stalls.

Some farmers allow their pigs to farrow naturally in outside huts or arks, and claim that crates are totally unnecessary. Others agree with more old-fashioned pig-farming books, which justify the use of farrowing crates during the first 48-72 hours of piglets' lives.[9]

Nowadays, however, greater intensification has led to their much wider use. It has become increasingly common to keep sows in crates for two or three weeks and then to take piglets away from them. In natural conditions, weaning takes approximately two months.

Leaving aside for a moment possible traumas associated with such practices for the young, let us first examine early weaning from the mother's viewpoint. During the period that she is producing most milk for her piglets, her young are separated from her. This deprivation of maternal instinct is not eased by any medication to stop milk flow, as might be administered to a human mother unable or unwilling to feed her baby. Such treatment amounts to uneconomic expenditure when withdrawal of food and water for 24 hours will harden up her milk without monetary outlay. Soreness endured by the mother pig is simply ignored since it has no detrimental long-term economic effects. (Of course, it would be pure sentimentality to assume that all sows enjoy suckling their young, particularly when their whole lives consist of continuous cycles of pregnancy, farrowing and lactation. On the contrary, it must often represent something of an endurance test.)

As soon as piglets are removed, the sows are returned to their confinement stall. In a further five to seven days, when they show signs of coming back into heat, they are once again served by the boar and the whole reproductive cycle repeats itself. Now that adoption of early weaning allows breeding females to be inseminated five weeks earlier than before, it has become possible to produce five litters every two years, instead of the traditional four.

According to the National Farmers' Union survey already mentioned, 'the steadily growing popularity of three-week weaning (in practice between 17 and 25 days) is evidenced by the fact that one-third of producers now use this system'. A small percentage of farmers have gone one step further and wean their piglets in less than 17 days. For early-weaned piglets, a number of systems are available, the most intensive being 'piggiboxes'. These are environmentally-controlled cages, often in two or three tiers. Temperature is maintained at around 85°C, stocking densities are high and floors are usually made of perforated or punched metal to allow easy dung collection from a slurry pit beneath. No separate area is provided. Run along similar principles are 'flat-deck' cages, where piglets are once again kept on metal slatted floors without separate dunging areas.

A quick glance through pig industry journals will confirm that there is no single accepted method of keeping early-weaned piglets. Advertisements abound, stressing the virtures of this or that contraption, most of them striking the disinterested reader as wholly inappropriate to the needs of playful young creatures. Leaving aside the minority of exceptions which allow adequate space and environment, the same problems always arise. The environment is barren, stocking densities are too high and floors (concrete or slats) are unsuitable for cloven-hoofed four-legged animals.

Impoverished conditions create several management difficulties. Normally, these are solved by mutilations. For instance, tail-biting is prevalent amongst fattening pigs, so most stock have their tails docked in the first few days of their lives. How far this should be necessary is another contentious subject in the pig farming world. Back in 1965, the Brambell Report (para. 124) offered the following assessment, which still seems relevant:

> Docking is becoming increasingly common with the spread of intensive methods. It is practised as a matter of routine on all pigs intended for fattening in some premises, but in others it is resorted to only when vice occurs in a particular batch. We believe that the vice of tail-biting is rare under good management in suitable houses that are not overstocked, and that in consequence docking will be generally unnecessary under the conditions we have specified. We disapprove of this mutilation in principle, it involves the destruction of sensitive tissue and bone, thus causing severe pain and we recommend that the docking of pigs should be prohibited, save when necessary as a remedial treatment by a veterinary surgeon.

These recommendations have been totally ignored, like so much of the report.

Another common mutilation is castration. This operation is inflicted upon young male pigs because the meat industry insists that the flesh of male pigs is marred by what is known as 'boar-taint'[10] giving an unpleasant flavour to the meat. Many, including the National Pig Breeding Association, believe this is 'a bit of a myth'. They argue that pigs for bacon and pork are now fattened up for slaughter so quickly that there is no time for them to develop boar-taint. (Bacon pigs are slaughtered at 5-6 months old; pork pigs at 18-22 weeks). Yet castration remains an accepted practice for male pigs, usually performed by the pig keeper in the first few days of life.

Whether or not they have been early-weaned in flat-deck cages, or weaned naturally at 2 months and kept in reasonable condition, almost all fattening pigs are reared intensively during the last weeks of their short lives. Worst of all are 'sweat-boxes' where pigs are exceptionally tightly packed into a small space. Buildings are unheated, the idea being that high temperature and humidity are maintained by the pigs' body-weight. The animals lie in their own filth and even pick their food out of it. As with many intensive fattening units, food is merely scattered over the floor from mechanical dispensers overhead. One or two large producers confess to still using sweat-boxes.

Most fattening pens consist of concrete floors, with a separate dunging area. In the best of them, straw and some natural ventilation are supplied. Nevertheless, overcrowding, dim lighting and inadequate floor surfaces are very common, as are unsatisfactory feeding arrangements and inadequate dunging facilities. The revised codes of practice recommend that 'the total floor space should be adequate for sleeping, feeding and exercising',[11] and that 'minimum sleeping areas, excluding dunging areas, should be of sufficient size to accommodate all the pigs in the pen lying on their sides'. At present, these codes of practice are sometimes blatantly ignored, in which case there is no room for all pigs to lie down in their pen at the same time.

Another feature of intensification that the pig industry has in common with its poultry counterpart is proliferation of disease. For example, since the first outbreak in 1972, there have been 500 outbreaks of swine vesicular disease. In 1980 alone, there were 60 outbreaks, forcing compulsory slaughter of 47,118 pigs.[12] Swine vesicular disease is a virus usually associated with 'swill feeding of pigs or to the movement of pigs from infected to clean premises'.

Another virus, Aujesky's disease, kills piglets, causes sows to abort and temporary sterility in boars. The incidence has increased enormously in recent years and some believe it 'poses a serious threat to the British pig herd'.[13]

In the winter of 1980, 100 farms reported outbreaks of transmissible gastro-enteritis amongst young pigs. The symptoms are inflamed stomachs and diarrhoea, sometimes with ulceration and bleeding.[14]

In 1981, a fresh outbreak of streptococcal meningitis was reported at 10-12 per cent of all pig units in East Anglia. Unheard of in this country before 1970, it is said to be caused by mixing and moving unweaned piglets and is fatal in 50 per cent of cases. The disease can be transferred to humans, sometimes causing permanent deafness.

Vets and abattoir workers are particularly susceptible.[15]

Oedema disease is stress-related. Piglets become susceptible to infection in response to abnormal pressures, such as overcrowding, mixing of groups, prolonged journeys, rough handling, lack of trough space, and so on. One research scientist estimates that it has killed 4,000 young pigs over the last seven years. His findings show that incidence 'increased dramatically' when piggiboxes and flat-decks were introduced, and 'is causing increasing numbers of deaths in weaners'.[16]

Respiratory diseases are also rampant. One vet who has made a study of the problem is M.R. Muirhead. He has estimated that 'up to 70 per cent of bacon-weight pigs show evidence' of enzootic pneumonia.[17] Stressing that disease increases with greater intensification, he adds,

> In large herds, where the cubic capacity of the fattening houses is reduced to maintain temperatures and large numbers of pigs are housed in a common air space, the levels of clinical pneumonia can be high with up to 2-3 per cent under treatment at any one time.[18]

A further revealing comment on the proliferation of disease on pig farms comes from Dr David Sainsbury in the January 1982 edition of *Pig Farming*:

> A high incidence of modern diseases and sub-clinical infections are due to bacteria and other organisms that normally live in small numbers in the animal in reasonable harmony with their surroundings, producing ill effect when the challenge is too great to be withstood.[19]

A recent Ministry of Agriculture film quotes a survey of slaughterhouses which concludes that 55 per cent of pigs slaughtered suffer from nasal deformities; 27 per cent from infected livers, and 30 per cent from enzootic pneumonia. The average loss of production on pig farms is put at 10 per cent.[20]

Foot and leg injuries due to unsatisfactory floor surfaces are simply accepted by the industry, since they do not cause mortality amongst fattening stock. A survey of the hoof horns of 2,000 pork pigs examined at the slaughter house of Budapest Meat Industry Enterprise found that 85.1 per cent were unhealthy.[21] (Those who would argue that what happens in Hungary is not applicable to pig farming here would do well to consider why the authors of that survey were invited to read their paper at a Pig Veterinary Society meeting in the UK.)

Leg injuries also widely affect breeding stock. According to a Meat and Livestock Commission investigation, almost 12 per cent of sows were slaughtered because of lameness.[22] Apart from failure to breed and advanced age, this represents the most common reason for culling.

## Veal production

Unlike their European counterparts, the British public have never been great eaters of veal. The French eat an estimated 40 times as much as we do and the Italians 20 times more. Exact figures are hard to come by since the Ministry of Agriculture combine veal production with other methods of calf rearing, but according to the secretary of the British Veal Association, about 30,000 calves a year are reared for veal in this country. In addition, at least the same number again are imported from Holland. To quote the Ministry of Agriculture, 'large unit production of veal got under way in this country some 30 years ago when suitably fortified skim milk powder was produced as a by-product in the dairy industry'.[23]

Until recently, almost all veal calves were reared in narrow crates. Details of this appalling system were so widely publicized, however, that sales were severely restricted. Consequently, in 1980, Britain's largest retail producers, Quantock Veal Ltd, ripped out their veal crates and changed over to more humane straw-yards. They did so, freely admitting that veal had become 'a four-letter word' to the public and that there had been no possibility of expansion whilst the stamp of cruelty was associated with the product.

Nevertheless, despite Quantock's claim to control a large proportion of this country's retail veal market, at least 30-40 per cent, probably more, of our 30,000 veal calves are still reared in crates.[24] These calves still live out their short lives in a system that the managing director of Quantock Veal Ltd described as 'morally repugnant'.

The first stage in crated veal production is to separate calves from their mothers when they are a few days old and put them in wooden stalls, slatted to allow dung and urine to fall down into a dropping pit beneath.

At about 2 weeks old, calves would normally start to take solid food. Like all ruminant animals, young cattle crave fibrous foods to satisfy their digestive needs. In intensive veal units, however, they are denied solids and are fed on a completely liquid milk diet, consisting of milk substitute compound with added chemicals, vitamins, minerals and disease-preventing drugs. Feeds are still based upon the EEC surplus skim milk powder.

This diet helps to produce pale-coloured 'white veal' − the flesh of calves kept deliberately short of iron and suffering from anaemia. No meat from ruminant animals is naturally white.

Temperature and high humidity are maintained within the veal house to stimulate the calves into drinking plenty of fattening milk-gruel. Water, which is far more thirst-quenching, is denied for the same reason. Total-milk diets promote diarrhoea, and runny faeces make slats wet and slippery, as well as extremely uncomfortable.

Calves become desperate for iron and will go to the lengths of licking their own urine, gnawing wooden crates and licking their own hair, in an attempt to obtain it. Huge hair balls are sometimes removed from calves' stomachs after slaughter.

Other aspects of their living conditions are equally repugnant. After 3 weeks or so, calves grow too large to turn around in their narrow crates and are unable to groom themselves properly. The environment is kept as barren as possible in order to minimize the amount of 'damage' that can be done by calves searching for iron.

Veal crates allow calves one choice. They can either stand up or half lie down. Changing over from one position to the other involves using knee joints, which tend to become swollen from the dual effects of dampness and lack of exercise.

After 14 weeks or so in narrow crates, usually in dim light and allowed to put their heads through the front of the crate only at feeding times, these sickly, pathetic creatures are taken off for slaughter. Many are barely able to walk. Ulcers, chronic diarrhoea, respiratory problems, pneumonia and septicaemia are all management problems in factory veal units, and despite the early slaughter age, they are controlled only by widespread medication.

The British Veal Association claims that no new veal producer utilizes crates, but admits that all imported veal from Holland derives from factory farms, as well as 10,000 or more calves produced in this country, already mentioned.

There is one other way in which Britain contributes to the suffering of veal calves. Every year, we export between 200,000 and 300,000 calves to other EEC countries. At the end of their long journeys most of these animals end their lives in continental crated veal units.

## Beef and dairy cattle

Factory farming has not taken the same kind of hold over other kinds of livestock production. For instance, even though killing ages of beef cattle have continued to fall, and some are now slaughtered as early as 11 months without ever seeing pasture, we have yet to imitate truly the American example of mammoth-scale beef-lots, where cattle are often packed closely into concrete yards without shelter. The majority of beef farming, like sheep rearing, at least bears some relation to farming systems of old.

Similar comments could be offered about dairy farming. The majority of herds are still allowed outside onto pasture in warmer months and are housed in barns or sheds during winter. Obviously, much depends upon the quality of both the pasture and the indoor facilities provided, but given that these allow sufficient space, food, bedding, etc, they provide an environment which is at least basically suitable to cattle. Nevertheless, there do remain several disturbing trends in dairy farming.

Although the actual number of dairy cows kept in this country has remained fairly static over the last decade (at the end of 1981 the figure was 3,295,000)[25] there have been considerable increases in the size of herds. Whilst the average herd size is still under 100 cows, farms with more than 100, or even 200, are relatively common.

This growth has created several welfare problems, notably during the winter months. In the past, herds were normally brought indoors during the worst weather in order to avoid pasture damage. Environment varied from farm to farm, but typically cows were kept in covered barns or yards and mucked out daily. The straw provided manure.

A combination of factors now conspire against this well-tried system. In particular, labour has been greatly reduced and straw has become expensive. Add to this the increased difficulty of mucking out large herds of 100 or more cows, and the sort of difficulties presented are not hard to imagine. These range from discomfort and smell, to sewage disposal and drainage. Farmers have tried many types of bedding in an attempt to defeat the problem of regular mucking out. Straw, wood shavings and peat have all been tried. Some have even gone so far as to use slatted floors. Bare concrete is quite common.

Despite widespread experimentation, one difficulty remains: unless the shed is cleared frequently an accumulation of dung from 100 or so cows can soon become knee-deep. Apart from aesthetic considerations, health is also affected. Walking on abrasive floors can cause lameness; and standing in slurry can lead to softening of the horn, which subsequently becomes prone to invasion by infectious agents. Such environments are also breeding grounds for udder infections since large amounts of dung are likely to come into close contact with udders and teats. All these problems are on the increase.

Another disquieting practice which may become more prevalent if herds continue to grow in size, is zero-grazing (i.e. not allowing cattle to graze at all). Obviously, as more cows are kept, more land is needed to feed them adequately. Eventually, the point is reached where the most feasible method of feeding is to sow the fields to intensive grasses and then take food to the beasts in the form of silage added to concentrated feeds. As yet, only a small number of zero-grazing herds are kept in this country, but there are no laws to prevent its adoption on a wider scale.

A cause for greater concern is an increasing interference with the reproductive life of dairy cows. Artificial insemination is now responsible for at least 60 per cent of all conceptions; the practice of embryotomy (where the newly conceived foetus of 'high quality' cows is transferred to the womb of less productive beasts in an attempt to ensure more profitable young); mating young heifer cows at increasingly early ages (between 18 months and 2 years); genetic breeding to promote abnormally high milk yields and milking three times a day: all these practices are both gaining in popularity and creating new welfare problems. Embryotomy and early mating often lead to painful and protracted births, since the calf may grow too big inside the womb for the mother to give birth in relative comfort; higher-yielding cows sometimes have enormous udders, often swinging near to the ground and therefore more prone to infections like mastitis.[26]

The search for greater milk yields (i.e. more profit) also affects the life of the cow after she gives birth. It is one of the unavoidable cruelties of dairy production that the calf is taken away from its mother at an early age so that the milk which nature intended for the young can be diverted to the dairy. In a bid to extract every drop of milk, it is common for the calf to be removed as soon as possible, after it has taken its mother's first milk. (The first milk, known as colostrum, contains various antibodies vital for the calf's protection against ill-health.)

A number of possible fates await new-born calves, depending upon both breeding and quality. They may be reared on to beef, sold as a British veal calf, or exported at about 30 days old to a continental veal unit. Some females may become dairy herd replacements and a few males are kept as breeding bulls. The least healthy calves are sent via market straight to the slaughterhouse to be used mainly in pet foods or for rennett and other by-products.

Although most dairy cows enjoy a better life than factory-farmed pigs and chickens, it could be argued that the only reason for this is that, hitherto, it has not proved economically worthwhile to keep them similarly confined. Even though we have not yet seriously imitated the US dairy industry, where approximately 50 per cent of cows are kept permanently confined in intensive units,[27] the same principle of using technology primarily as a ruthless source of profit is evident to some degree. Where might it lead us in the future?

# 3. To the slaughter

Marketing, transport and slaughter is always, to varying degrees, an ordeal for farm animals. Separated from their familiar environment and often from their normal companions, they are under stress and easily frightened. It is a time that demands sensitive and patient handling, yet, as in the case of poultry transport and slaughter, these qualities are often lacking.

## Markets

The best thing to be said for livestock markets is that at least they are open to public scrutiny. Anybody under the impression that the picture of violent treatment of animals presented here is biased or uninformed, would do well to mingle inconspicuously with farmers, drovers, auctioneers and dealers on a few market days. The chances are that they will witness considerable suffering.

There are approximately 500 livestock auction markets in Great Britain. Some 60 per cent of cattle slaughtered, 70 per cent of sheep and 12 per cent of pigs pass through them, plus a good many poultry and rabbits.[1] Rather than present another dossier of the numerous individual examples of brutality reported, it is sufficient for our present purposes to summarize the sort of problems that exist. Any concerned reader can always test personally the validity of this case.

One of the chief problems at markets is that inadequate facilities sometimes result in overcrowded pens, or difficulties in loading, unloading and moving animals to and from the auction ring. Many drovers employ violent implements like goads with nails in the end, or else use electric goads in sensitive areas in order to prod frightened animals to the right place. Loading tends to become particularly brutal towards the end of the day, when the combined effects of frustration, anxiousness to get home and alcohol (bars are usually open long hours on market days), lead to increasingly short tempers. It is then that one is most likely to witness kicking and beating, or young animals being lifted onto lorries by their ears and legs and thrown about (especially if the RSPCA market official is not about to supervise). Although the Markets (Protection of Animals) Order (1964) makes certain welfare provisions for procedures, these are often blatantly ignored. Water should always be available; sometimes it is not. Horned and unhorned animals should not be mixed; sometimes they are.

There are many disturbing sights at most markets: accepted mutilations like ear punching; the overcrowded crates in which rabbits and poultry are kept; the rough handling of pigs, or 'barren cows', repaid in violence for years of profitable milk production. (These normally placid animals are then sold off to processed meat factories). But no animals appear more pathetic than the sickly young calves, made to endure the ordeal of the auction ring before being sent to the slaughterhouse, usually for pet food; or the dealers' calves, arriving at market exhausted after being hawked around two or three auctions in a week. To its credit, Rugby Market recently announced a ban on this latter practice, giving this explanation for the decision: 'Mr Young knew of calves which, bought in Norwich on a Saturday, were presented at Rugby on Monday, Melton Mowbray on Tuesday and Banbury on Wednesday. In some instances they were not even taken off the transport overnight.[2] The British Veterinary Association have suggested that it should be an offence to present calves for sale at more than one market in 28 days; even the NFU are opposed to calf hawking. Yet for all the talk, no action has yet been taken to curb the trade on a national level.

## Transport of animals

The trade which tends to be most strongly associated with cruelty to animals during transportation is the live export of food animals for further fattening and slaughter. It is not difficult to see why. Despite repeated exposés of excessive hardship endured in transit to the continent, official sources continue to defend this miserable traffic with hollow words and equally hollow legislation. Meanwhile every year, thousands of consignments are sent on needlessly long journeys across the Channel in order to provide quick profit for a few farmers, dealers and transporters.

The live export trade is irreconcilable with humane treatment of animals. It is as simple as that. On statistical grounds alone, animals are prone to acts of human brutality and negligence. The longer the journey, the more checks required. Consequently the animals are under greater stress, more human beings are needed to handle them, and more human patience and sympathy is required. It is a vicious circle which goes a long way to explaining how reports of brutality have been voiced repeatedly over the years.

In opposition to criticism, the Ministry of Agriculture argue that what we might call the dubious principles of live exports, can be neutralized by adequate legislation. As a result, the last decade has seen a steady stream of paper regulations at both national and EEC level, designed to control the trade. Britain's latest effort was the Live Export Order (1981), whilst the EEC directive on the international transport of animals, limits journeys to a maximum of 24 hours. Yet even though this latter directive falls well short of Britain's domestic law (which forbids travel for more than 12 hours), it is still frequently ignored.

The *News of the World* of 21 March 1982, in conjunction with the Dartmoor Livestock Protection Society,[3] reported on a consignment of 500 sheep followed on the Calais ferry from Dover. The Channel crossing was made during a gale; at Calais the animals were transferred from two British lorries onto a four-tier French transporter, crowded to the extent that the driver had to prod them with a pole to pack them all in. Then, they were driven all night in torrential, drenching rain. Eventually, 527 miles from Calais, they arrived at the abattoir in the village of Prudhomat. They had travelled for 25 hours since their last drink of water. Many were in a state of collapse. Others were biting each other's wool and pawing the ground from the effects of hunger, thirst and stress. This is not an isolated example. On the contrary, almost every new investigation reveals blatant infringements of the law, with calves or sheep travelling for more than 24 hours without feed or water.

Since there is no EEC police force, it is patently obvious that no EEC directive carries any real authority. Indeed our own government, whilst on the one hand defending live exports, are at the same time forced to admit that 'we have no jurisdiction over animals on foreign soil'.[4] Although the ministry try to justify their position by arguing further that strict veterinary control is maintained, it is impossible to take such suggestions seriously when, by the end of 1981, no consignment of commercial food animals had been accompanied from this country to final destination by official veterinary staff since 1975.

Apart from the cruelty of transportation, there is much concern over the conditions which our farm animals find when they reach their destination. For example, most of the calves exported from this country go to continental veal units. Quoting once again the words of Philip Paxman, managing director of Quantock Veal, 'some of the facts are none too pleasant, with calves often reared in darkness and with no opportunity for play or herd behaviour'.

The fate of those animals transported for immediate slaughter is also controlled (in word anyway) by an EEC directive. Even supposing that this is adhered to, it falls well short of British standards. Moreover, the directive is often ignored. There are frequent reports of animals bled to death whilst fully conscious in France and Italy. Furthermore, the problem is bound to intensify as the EEC gains new members. For instance, in Spain the 'puntilla' method of slaughter is still commonplace. Basically, this consists of tying the unfortunate animal to rings in the wall, or trapping its head between two adjustable bars. It is then killed by a long narrow knife thrust down at the back of the head. No doubt, when Spain officially joins the EEC and we begin to send animals there, our ministry will claim that such slaughter methods cannot be utilized by member states. But what real assurances will we have that our animals will not meet a barbaric end at the close of their journey?

To point to the inadequacies of some foreign slaughterhouses is not to suggest that British slaughter conditions are always better than their continental counterparts. Rather, it is to illustrate that the only way we can take full responsibility for transportation and slaughter is to kill animals whilst we retain full jurisdiction over their fate. On welfare grounds, it is imperative that we abide by stated policy of the British Veterinary Association that animals should be slaughtered as near to the point of departure as is possible. Live exports are inconsistent with such a policy.

What makes the live export trade even more unforgivable is that it makes no sense whatsoever on economic grounds either.[5] Every day we import meat products worth something in the region of £3½ million. The income from the live export trade in a year totals only enough to pay for our imported meat and meat preparations for four or five days. Moreover, it is not as if there is opposition to the export of meat and meat products. With modern chilled lorries, it is perfectly possible to export meat on the hook to all points of Europe. As well as saving our animals needless suffering this would also create work in our own abattoirs, and in the trades that deal with animal by-products, like tanneries.

Why then do live exports continue, encouraged by successive governments? Yet again, it is evident that the profits of a minority are being given priority over the interests of the majority of both humans and farm animals. The live export regime suits our dairy farmers whose surplus calves often fetch a better price from continental veal farmers than on our own market, and it also suits sheep farmers who according to EEC subsidies sometimes receive financial incentives to export animals alive. Equally, it is to the benefit of vast chains of dealers and transporters, who capitalize on the shifting of animals. But it is not practised for the economic benefit of the nation, or the welfare advantage of cows and sheep. A ban on the live export trade is imperative. It is not scare-mongering to warn that if the trade continues and the EEC expands, then in future, we will see still greater numbers of animals sent abroad and travelling greater distances. I quote National Farmers' Union member and transport owner, D.L. Parker:

> The liberalization of trade between the EEC partners will, through the interplay of market forces, encourage more movement of animals. We will have to face up to these changes. No longer can the transport of animals to the continent be looked upon as an 'export exercise' — but it is normal trade within a business community... [This] will probably increase in both numbers and extent.[6]

Customs and excise figures show that in 1982, 233,665 calves and 140,164 sheep and lambs were exported from the UK for further fattening and slaughter. Over 500,000 pigs and 50,000 adult cattle were also sent overseas, making a total of more than 1 million animals.

## Domestic transportation

Focusing so much attention upon the live export trade has one unfortunate consequence: people assume that this means that our domestic trade is perfectly acceptable. This is not the case; it also leaves much to be desired.

Advanced technology has provided us with sophisticated vehicles capable of transporting perishable goods over long distances, at whatever temperature, humidity, etc., is most appropriate to the particular product. Yet generally speaking, live animals are not considered sufficiently 'perishable' to warrant controlled conditions that might minimize the stress of transportation. Little effort has been made to improve animal transporters over the years and many 'primitive' problems are still common. These range from lack of ventilation, to overcrowding, unsuitable slippery floors, poor suspension, double-decker lorries where the faeces from the top layer fall directly on top of those below (in the case of sheep three-tier lorries are still common), and poorly designed loading and unloading ramps.[7] This latter problem obviously increases the likelihood of brutality when getting animals on and off lorries.

Pigs are particularly susceptible to damage during transportation; 56 per cent of carcases were found to be damaged in one survey conducted by the Meat and Livestock Commission.[8] Most of the damage was attributable to handling of the live animal during transport, according to a Ministry of Agriculture official.[9] Another survey records 10 per cent of all lambs damaged by bad handling.[10] Furthermore, animals nowadays face increasingly long journeys to slaughterhouses. Fat pigs may travel from Scotland to the North and Midlands, or from East Anglia to the South West; and fat sheep from Wales to the South West and Midlands.[11] Long distances increase the probability of stress.

There is no doubt that the technical expertise needed to minimize these problems already exists; all that is lacking is the concern. Not until it can be proved that the considerable financial losses from bruising and stress is great enough to warrant investment will the industry act.

## Slaughterhouses

The nature of slaughterhouses has changed considerably in recent years, almost as much as farms themselves. In the past, almost every small town had at least one small slaughterhouse and many animals were actually killed at the back of the butcher's shop. By today's standards most abattoirs killed comparatively few animals every year. The trend now is towards fewer and larger slaughterhouses, with factory-type processing lines. In 1981, there were 1,135 abattoirs in the UK. Small abattoirs had decreased by 775 over the previous decade, whilst those killing between 50,000 and 100,000 cattle each year had shown an increase.[12]

Control over hygiene, welfare and meat quality in slaughterhouses is in the hands of meat inspectors, employed by local councils. The abattoir staff themselves work in gangs. Each member is allocated a particular task on the production line between bringing animals into the lairage (rest area) and packing them off to the retailers. Since slaughterhouses pay piece rates (i.e. according to the number of animals processed), there is considerable pressure on each member of the gang to maximize throughput in order to ensure financial advantage for the whole team. Slaughterers themselves receive no formal training. After a period working in the slaughterhouse they are considered qualified to slaughter and are given a licence to do so. According to the Slaughterhouse Act (1974) the official qualifications are 'a fit and proper person' and 'eighteen' years of age. It is indicative of our attitude to farm animals that whilst considerable sums are devoted to training meat inspectors, no similar investment for slaughterers is thought necessary.

The debate about ritual slaughter has dominated discussion about slaughter of animals in recent years. The Slaughterhouse Act (1974) allows Jews and Muslims to kill animals according to religious traditions, without stunning animals prior to slaughter. In Jewish slaughter, adult cattle are restrained in a holding pen and then rotated until they are upside down before the throat is cut. Sheep are placed upside down in a type of cradle; calves are either killed in the same way or hoisted by a back leg. Restraining and turning must prove terrifying to the victim. Muslims sometimes use the same methods or else lay the animals down on a bed of straw and hold the head manually.

It has proved difficult to campaign against ritual slaughter without inviting charges of racialism. Yet the fact remains that these practices are unacceptable on welfare grounds alone. Admirable though the concept of religious toleration is, it should not be extended to allow minorities to practice activities that are outlawed for the rest of the community on the grounds that they are too barbaric. Many enlightened Jews and Muslims share the opinion of protestors, who argue that any religious tradition which demands the death of animals without using every means available to minimize suffering, is mocking the name of true religion.[13] It is revealing that Iceland, Sweden, Norway, Switzerland and parts of Austria — countries with a reputation for advanced human rights and religious toleration — have all banned ritual slaughter.

One unfortunate effect of the mountain of publicity afforded to the ritual slaughter issue is that it has deflected attention from the atrocious conditions which often exist for farm animals which are stunned before their throats are cut. Despite enormous financial aid in recent years, the design of abattoirs is often poor.[14] Firstly, the lairage area (where animals are put to recover from the stress of their journey) is often inadequate, allowing insufficient ventilation and causing overcrowding. Sometimes groups of animals are mixed with 'strangers' causing stress or even fighting. Although the aim of the lairage is to present animals with quiet and comfortable conditions where they can settle down, in reality there is often noise, too much light or too many disturbances, which dispel any possibility of them quietening down before they are taken to their deaths.

When the time comes for slaughter itself, more problems of design frequently arise. The area between the lairage and stunning pen is known as the 'race'. Often 'races' have sharp bends or obstructions, making it extremely difficult to shift groups of already restless cows, pigs or sheep. The more troublesome the beasts become, then, once again, the more prone they are to acts of human brutality. One licensed slaughterer reports, 'Excessive use of electric goads is normal, as is tail twisting and sometimes tail breaking in an attempt to move reluctant animals. Extreme measures include scalding water poured over the rump or beating and poking with iron rods.'[15]

Of the three animals most commonly slaughtered, adult cattle probably have the best deal. They are moved individually into the stunning pen, where a holding apparatus keeps the head still so that the person in control of pre-stunning can shoot the cow with a captive bolt pistol[16] aimed at the forehead. Provided that poorly designed pens do not make it impossible for the slaughterers to shoot the animal accurately, most, though by no means all cattle will be stunned instantaneously. The holding pen is then opened and the beast falls on to the slaughterhouse floor below. From there, the animal may be pithed — a large stick is stirred around the hole made by the captive bolt pistol — before being shackled by a back leg and hoisted on to a conveyor belt for throat-slitting. The bleeding trough follows, after which the process of removing the inedible parts begins.

The most common method of stunning pigs in this country is through electrocution. Up to 20 pigs are driven into a stunning pen. When there are only small numbers involved, one man will usually be responsible for both stunning and hoisting, but where there is a large batch, a second may well be employed to hoist. The stunning operator greets the pigs with a pair of electric tongs, which are to be held over the temples of the pigs so that electricity passes through the brain and renders the animals insensitive to pain. Unfortunately, a number of factors often prevent the operation from working efficiently.

Firstly, despite provisos to the contrary, the equipment is not always regularly maintained. Tongs can become clogged with bits of hair. In time, this can act as insulation against the shock.

Secondly, whether or not the pigs know they are about to be slaughtered, they are inevitably disturbed and frightened by the sight of other animals falling to the floor immobile as a result of the tongs. Consequently, by the time the stunning operator reaches the last of any group of pigs, they are trying hard to evade him. In some circumstances, the frustrated human operator will then use his electric tongs across the backs of the animals, simply as a means to get at them properly.

Thirdly, the very nature of the factory process of modern slaughterhouses tends to work against proper stunning. The emphasis is always upon speed to maintain piecework rates. Each member of the gang knows only too well that delays will lead to criticism and abuse from the rest of the workforce. Therefore, corners tend to be cut. According to the Ministry of Agriculture recommendations, the electric tongs should be applied for a minimum of 7 seconds when, (as is usually the case) the voltage is low, at around 90 volts. In practice the stunning appartus is rarely applied for longer than 2 seconds. As a result, many experts believe that low-level electric stunning does not render pigs insensitive to pain. All it achieves is to make the animal immobile, so that it can be more easily hoisted on to the shackle line for 'sticking'. The brain may still be active.[17] Alternatively, it may take too long to 'stick' the animal after stunning, in which case, even when it has been stunned correctly, it will recover consciousness before the death-cut.

Why do they not simply turn up the electricity and kill the animals almost instantaneously? The principal explanation is much the same as with poultry. It is feared that high-voltage stunning may affect the quality of the carcase by stopping heartbeat before 'sticking'. The meat industry maintains that heart action is vital to successful 'bleeding' (i.e. draining blood from the corpse after the throat has been slit). Whether or not this is true is now open to doubt. Many members of the meat trade are questioning whether or not existing objections to high-voltage stunning are justified. In Holland, it is now widely used[18] and in this country a survey by the Meat Research Institute, has concluded that heart-stoppage does not damage meat quality.[19] As yet, however, few commercial enterprises have abandoned low-voltage stunning.

Sheep are also normally stunned by electric tongs, the thick covering of wool around the temples making the operation even more prone to failure than with pigs. Privately, some slaughterers express the view that approved methods merely result in the animal being tortured by electricity before stunning. As a result, the rules tend to be broken on both welfare and economic grounds. In the words of Dr Joe Gracey veterinary food hygienist, 'Do occasions occur when the throat is cut without prior stunning in sheep outside ritual slaughter?'[20] It seems likely that they do.

Conditions vary enormously within individual abattoirs, depending not only upon efficiency of equipment and adequate inspection, but also upon the attitude of the slaughterer himself. Surprisingly, some do maintain a sense of responsibility towards the animals that they kill, and do all that they can to ensure a quick and relatively painless death. Nevertheless, in order to slaughter animal after animal, day after day, it is normally necessary to repress any channels of human sympathy that might otherwise be brought to the task. For instance, one ex-slaughterer writes interestingly about his experiences, stressing the desensitizing nature of slaughterhouse work:

> I made my application for a licence and before I got it I had to prove myself. The first time I was asked to shoot a cow I couldn't do it. The thought of sending a bolt through its brain made me feel quite bad. I often thought, 'Why should I have the right to end a life?'
>
> I overcame the feeling by building up a hate for the animals I was going to kill. I was cruel in ways but not excessively. Animals know they are going to die and most will not walk to it as casually as people think.[21]

Ultimately, the concept of 'humane slaughter' is unachievable, since the two words are essentially incompatible. Nevertheless, it is possible to reduce the excessive torment inflicted upon many animals in British slaughterhouses. As the Ammedown Group puts it in their report, 'It is clear that there is much to be done about the humaneness of current methods of handling amongst animals destined for slaughter.'

# 4. Enter the health hazards

It is no exaggeration to say that without inputs from the pharmaceutical industry, factory farming would collapse in an epidemic of infectious diseases. Drug companies are beginning to see animal farming as a source of big profits. In 1977 alone, £54 million were spent on what are called 'animal health products' in the UK.[1] By 1980 the figure had risen to £80 million.[2] Most of the major multinational drug companies have now diversified their interests to incorporate the farming industry, amongst them ICI, Beechams, Ciba-Geigy, Hoechst, Fisons, Pfizer, the Wellcome Foundation, Upjohn, Glaxo, Eli Lilly and May & Baker. Farming magazines and trade journals are packed with advertisements extolling the virtues of a multitude of substances, as new drugs proliferate onto the market. Anti-stress sedatives; energy boosters to encourage animals to eat more; hormones to encourage speedy fattening, to regulate when animals give birth or to encourage conception rates, and antibiotics to fight mounting problems with disease: to the drug industry, factory farming is good news.

Almost all factory-farmed animals are fed regular doses of antibiotics, usually by adding to the feed. Low levels are normally administered to broiler chickens, battery hens, pigs, turkeys and veal calves. Quite simply, in the words of Dr David Sainsbury from the veterinary department at Cambridge University, 'the reasons for the greater need for antibiotics lies in the great increase in intensification'.[3] The sale of antibiotic drugs alone amounts to upwards of £20 million a year.[4]

Antibiotics fulfil a dual purpose. Partly, they act as a barrier against disease and stress. But more particularly, in animals fattened for eating they make a positive contribution towards growth rates. Nobody is certain how they work, but somehow they reduce the amount of feed needed to fatten animals up. The most likely explanation is that by reducing the levels of bacteria at certain points in the gut, antibiotics permit a greater uptake of food nutrients to go into weight gain. Normally, up to 40 per cent of food energy is taken up by bacteria living in the lower intestines. In the 1960s, when factory farming began its rapid expansion, concern over mounting drug abuse led to the setting up of a committee, instigated by government. The ensuing Swann Report (1969) attempted to overcome the problem by differentiating between drugs used in the treatment of disease and those administered to animals solely as growth promoters. The latter were allowed on free-sale under the title 'feed additives'; the former only on prescription. In addition, some disease-prevention drugs for the control of prevalent problems like blackhead and coccidiosis in poultry were also permitted on free-supply. In the long term the Swann Report has proved ineffective. The plan to prevent over-use of those substances with the potential to treat outbreaks of disease — known as therapeutic drugs — has failed, mainly because the environmental conditions in factory farms have created too many problems conducive to ill-health. As suggested by Dr Walton, research fellow at the veterinary department at Liverpool University, factory farming courts rampant disease: 'On most farms the scene was one of very young animals crowded together in constant contact with faeces and often with inadequate ventilation and temperature control.'[5] In response, therapeutic substances tend to be prescribed far more freely than was intended by the Swann Committee. For instance, we have only to look at the course of action recommended when enzootic pneumonia strikes at piggeries. (As we have seen already, one estimate puts the percentage of pigs affected at up to 70 per cent.) 'With the onset of coughing in any part of the system, in-feed medication with tetracycline 300/600g/ton... Short periods of water medication may also be required.'[6] Notice how the first sign of coughing results in *all* animals in the herd being treated with tetracycline, a drug also used to cure disease in humans. Even though tetracycline has to be prescribed by a veterinary surgeon, circumstances dictate that it is more or less freely available.

This proliferation creates several dangers to human health. The more often that any given antibiotic is used to treat a disease in animals, the more likely it is that the bacteria will develop resistance to it. Once resistance has been established, a comparatively mild strain may develop into a more virulent strain of bacterium which is not susceptible to the original antibiotic. Once this process begins, it can result eventually in the development of harmful (pathogenic) bacteria which are resistant to a variety of drugs, and infections which are therefore difficult to treat effectively. Moreover, this pattern can be transferred to the human consumer. Although progression does not run in such a straight line as shown in figure 4.1, there is indicated, nevertheless, some idea of the dangers.

Such a progression can be illustrated best by focusing upon salmonellosis, the most common bacterial infection amongst humans which is directly traceable to animals. Different strains of *Salmonella* thrive under all modern production methods. For instance, the British Veterinary Association has made the following comment about the broiler chicken industry: 'Having cheap poultry means hatching in large numbers, killing in large numbers, and breeding *Salmonella* in large numbers.'[7] In addition, Dr Patterson from Ross Poultry, one of Britain's largest chicken producers, has admitted that the huge numbers of birds slaughtered in each slaughter plant makes the problem of ensuring freedom form *Salmonella* 'an apparently insurmountable one'.[8] Between 30 per cent and 50 per cent of frozen chicken carcases are said to carry the bacteria.[9]

Minced meat is another potent source of *Salmonella*, with minced pigmeat particularly susceptible. This is probably due to the slaughter method, which allow 'infected faeces to splash onto the pig's skin'[10] and 'eventually reach the consumer's plate'.[11] Moving young calves through numerous markets is said to be chiefly responsible for a marked increase in a different strain of *Salmonella* bacteria. Weak calves, hawked about from market to market are particularly susceptible to invasion.

Despite the fact that most *Salmonella* bacteria are destroyed during cooking, in 1979/80, there were 19,452 reported cases of *Salmonella* food poisoning amongst Britain's human population. 'About two-thirds were attributable to intensive poultry and a further 20 per cent to other meat.'[12]

The potential dangers are greater than outbreaks of stomach poisoning. Once the process of transferable drug-resistance develops, then 'superbugs', unaffected by a whole range of antibiotics, may strike both animals and humans. Already, dangerous forms of

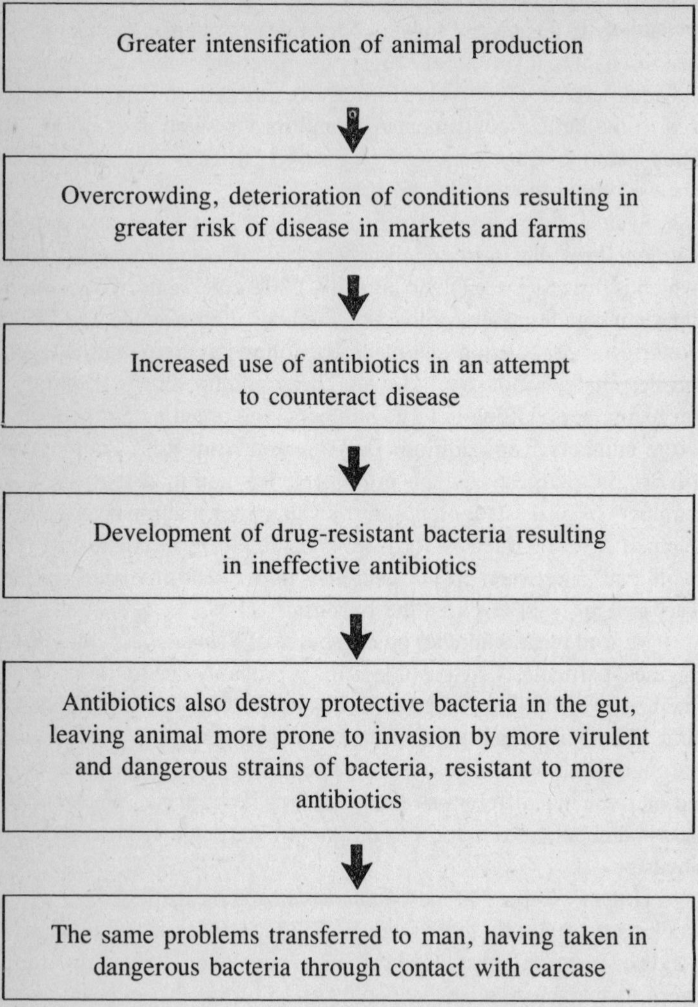

Greater intensification of animal production

Overcrowding, deterioration of conditions resulting in greater risk of disease in markets and farms

Increased use of antibiotics in an attempt to counteract disease

Development of drug-resistant bacteria resulting in ineffective antibiotics

Antibiotics also destroy protective bacteria in the gut, leaving animal more prone to invasion by more virulent and dangerous strains of bacteria, resistant to more antibiotics

The same problems transferred to man, having taken in dangerous bacteria through contact with carcase

*Figure 4.1* The dangers to human health from greater reliance upon drugs in animal farming

*Salmonella* have been sighted, particularly amongst calves. John Bell from the Central Veterinary Laboratory of the Ministry of Agriculture has had this to say about these 'new' bugs:

> At present none of these phage (bacteria) types is particularly dangerous to man. This is fortunate because if they were to acquire added virulence for man, we might be faced with an epidemic in food animals of a disease with the same potential for human illness as typhoid.[13]

In 1979, an outbreak of *Salmonella* resistant to eight major groups of drugs occurred on at least 50 farms in the South West, eventually causing 300 cases of enteric fever (typhoid organism) in humans, two of which proved fatal.[14] The *British Medical Journal* was convinced that the threat was initiated by a decision to allow more antibiotics in the treatment of disease in animals.[15] In particular, the use of trimethoprim, which is also one of the national health service's chief weapons in the event of an outbreak of typhoid organism, was condemned.[16] Added to the list of animal health products to counteract *Salmonella* in cattle, its effectiveness was quickly diminished by outbreaks of more virulent strains, totally resistant to it. The possible dangers to humans from this chain of events are evident.

Despite repeated warnings in farm and veterinary journals, no action has been introduced to curb the problem of over prescription of drugs. Some blame has been attached to the vets themselves for prescribing too freely, under pressure from their farming customers. According to some estimates, 60 per cent of their income is derived from the sale of drugs.[17] In response, the veterinary profession argue that the conditions under which animals are reared dictate that they utilize every means available, including administering drugs on a large scale.[18]

Meanwhile, competition for a share of the market in animal health medicines becomes increasingly competitive. Look through annual reports from all the big drug companies and there will almost certainly be some reference to the services that they intend to offer to agricultural progress. The Eli Lilly *Annual Report 1981* states:

> Modern agriculture will almost certainly top its past performance in the years ahead. Progress will come from an across-the-

board advance in agricultural science.

Elanco [name given to the agricultural side of the company] intends to share in this success through its established line of high-technology products, through newly developed compounds either recently marketed or now under field evaluation, and ultimately, through a research programme designed to generate breakthrough products in agriculture.

Apart from the established pharmeceutical companies, a thriving illicit trade also exists throughout Europe. Tactics employed by black marketeers have brought criticism from many quarters, including the official veterinary professsion.

The vets were unanimous in stressing that the answer was for farmers to buy their drugs through their vets. They shouldn't fall for all the special offers being touted around — transistor radios with sheep vaccines, rubber boots and anoraks with some medicaments and clocks and frying pans with others.[19]

With the black market now controlling an estimated 4 per cent of antibiotic sales on farms in the UK[20] it is increasingly difficult to keep any record of the substances employed as animal production aids.

It is not only antibiotics that are commonly sold to farmers. Figures estimate that between 25 per cent and 30 per cent of cattle are treated with hormones designed to improve feed conversion rates.[21] These work by interfering with natural development. As a rule, females are given male hormones, males are implanted with female hormones and steers with both.[22] Often these substances are implanted behind the ear by farmers and farmworkers, without veterinary supervision.[23]

Many people believe that these hormones carry health risks to humans. In September 1980, a French consumer group called for a complete boycott on the sale of veal because of the presence of growth-promoting hormones. It was alleged that these have links with cancer.[24] Soon after this incident, an Italian judge ordered a total ban on veal sales throughout his country. This followed a court case in which it was proved that calves had been treated with dangerous growth promoters. Subsequent checks ordered by the judge confirm- ed the presence of hormones in both imported and Italian veal. Traces were also discovered in baby foods.[25]

As a result, the EEC agricultural ministers initiated an investiga- tion, under considerable pressure from some member states to an- nounce a total ban on the use of growth promoting hormones in the rearing of livestock. Because of considerable opposition from other interested parties, however, a compromise emerged from the in- vestigations. The use of two groups of hormones was forbidden after July 1982, whilst others are still permitted. For the record, the ban- ned substances are known as stilbenes and thyrostatic drugs. Previous to the EEC ruling the former had been used widely in this country.

All drugs purchased legally carry details of withdrawal periods before slaughter, when the substances should not be applied. But there is concern that these are sometimes not adhered to, partly because of inadequate monitoring: 'There is a proportion of [pig] herds which have need to incorporate drugs throughout the finishing stages and there appears to be little in the way of checking that withdrawal has been practised.'[26] The current situation, where the feed or drug com- pany is responsible for presenting withdrawal times on labels, and the farmer is responsible for action, does not invite confidence.

The meat industry argues that there is no scientific evidence to prove that any of the growth promoters used in British livestock pro- duction are dangerous to human health. Yet such assurances must be treated with some scepticism when, at the same time, members of the Meat Research Institute admit that they are not even certain how drugs work, let alone what their effect may be in the long term. To quote Dr Perry, from MRI, producers are 'playing chemical roulette'[27] in an attempt to increase profits. Even where the rules governing permitted use of growth promoters and therapeutic medicines are obeyed, it is evident that methods of animal produc- tion dependent upon the pharmaceutical industry offer dangerous repercussions for human health, not to mention the effects of illegal- ly purchased substances, haphazard dosing and failure to apply withdrawal periods accurately.

Other health dangers are created after animals are slaughtered. Despite apparently thorough meat inspectorate systems in both poultry and red-meat slaughterhouses, hazards persist. In poultry processing, the speed of the conveyor belt means that in the time it takes an inspector to remove a diseased carcase from the line, it is quite possible for another to slip through. Also, the sheer monotony of working on the fast moving slaughter line for long periods makes close concentration extremely difficult. In red-meat abattoirs, a report on hygiene by the Meat Research Institute concludes that 'apparently effective cleaning procedures, such as washing or shearing an animal before slaughter, give only an illusion of hygiene, and actually have only a trivial effect on the level of contamination on the carcase'.[28] A more major source of contamination comes from the fact that meat handlers often cut successive carcases with the same knive. With all the meat also passing on the same surfaces, 'there is clearly a risk of spreading contamination'.[29]

Preservatives also play a part in meat production. Nitrites and nitrates are added routinely to all cured meats,[30] despite their association with cancer. Polyphosphates — basically salt solution — is injected into chicken carcases to prevent deterioration and improve 'ratings for flavour, tenderness and juiciness'.[31] Certainly, the meat industry never spoke a greater truth than when they chose as their advertising slogan, 'meat's got the lot'!

# 5. Human violence and animal suffering

From the discussion of the main methods of production that fit into the category of factory farming, it can be seen that whilst specific practices vary considerably — some animals are kept in near or total darkness, others under prolonged bright light; some animals are given drugs to promote fertility whilst others are fed them to retard sexual development, and so on — there is nevertheless, an overall philosophy behind all systems. The aim is to use every applicable development in science and technology to obtain as much animal produce as possible in return for the smallest investment. According to this ethos, welfare only becomes relevant when the physical well-being of a whole 'crop' of animals deteriorates to the point where mortality threatens profitability.

The most pertinent word to characterize these systems is 'violent'. But what is violence in agriculture? What makes factory farming so much more detestable than traditional methods of rearing animals for food? Demonstrably, it would be pure sentimentality to assume that all non-intensive farming was, or is, simply an idyllic picture of cows, pigs and chickens bounding freely around green fields, enjoying life to the limit of their potential. Considerable violence existed in agriculture long before factory methods took over, with practices like castration and permanent tethering of milch cows in city dairies destroying the idyllic image. Futhermore, the phrase 'free-range' can be used to cover a multitude of conditions and in its way a few animals cramped into an over-used, muddy patch is every bit as unacceptable as a battery farm. Ultimately, it is a fact that however good the living conditions, the very nature of animal rearing demands some violence — slaughter itself, the relatively early death of all animals and the forced separation of mother from young.

On the other hand, we should also acknowledge some positives in traditional farming. When the living conditions are suitable to the needs of the particular animal, and stocking methods are good, there is something to be admired in the sense of companionship and trust that can be established between humans and animals  and in both living life at something akin to a natural pace, according to and in touch with the seasons. Given a day to travel around the British countryside, we could all still witness scenes that would impress us by what we might call their naturalness. Scenes such as piglets or calves running with their mothers, animals responding to the farmer's call to feeding, or young animals at play together. These are valued features of non-intensive farming and they should lead us to distinguish it from battery production. Despite a degree of violence, at its best it is not wholly based upon violence.

Basically, there are three kinds of violence that can be inflicted upon farm animals — brutality, negligence and deprivation. Brutality usually involves an act of physical oppression, such as kicking or beating. As we have seen, brutality features in modern farming during marketing, transport and slaughter and in certain practices like debeaking of hens, where livestock are mutilated in an attempt to compensate for the inadequacies of the system employed. On the whole, however, factory farming is not characterized by this particular kind of violence. Animals in cages are not beaten or physically attacked by humans.

Similar comments could be applied to negligence. Is it any more negligent not to supply adequate ventilation or water or fire alarms in a battery unit on a hot summer day, than it is to leave sheep unattended without any attempt to provide either food or shelter on a wild mountainside during prolonged winter blizzards? Both result from negligent stocking methods and both are to be condemned. Fortunately, both are also comparatively rare. Within the limits of the system, most farmers do their best to provide their animals with the basics for survival. It is in their interests to do so.

It is in the third kind of cruelty, deprivation, that factory farming varies so radically from 'free-range'. Although it is not ostensibly brutal or negligent, it is inevitably cruel in that it deprives sentient animals of the opportunity to exercise their natural behaviour patterns or live their lives in anything remotely resembling a suitable environment. For instance, observations of pigs on free-range have revealed that they will spend up to six hours of every day rooting. They do so not only in search of food, but also out of inquisitiveness. The pig's snout is its chief centre of sensory perception so that when they take objects into their mouths, as they often will, they are frequently expressing natural curiosity, and not simply looking for food. In sow stalls, pigs spend 24 hours a day in solitary confinement, often on a floor of uncomfortable concrete without bedding; there is nothing to root amongst and no possibility of turning around, let alone of taking proper exercise. Research has shown that pigs are every bit as intelligent as cats or dogs, but if a dog or cat were to be deprived in a similar fashion it would constitute cruelty to animals under British law. Confine a pig in a narrow crate, often permanently tethered, and you may well qualify for some kind of financial assistance! This double standard, applied equally to other farm animals, exemplifies the kind of violence unavoidable in modern farming methods. Living creatures are deprived of even their most fundamental rights, such as movement and exercise. Only those factors which influence productivity are considered.

As well as causing immeasurable suffering to animals, this type of violence also says a great deal about our own human response to life. Perhaps this can be illustrated best by saying that in one sense there is less brutality in the rearing of factory-farmed animals than under traditional systems, for the simple reason that the very nature of the methods prohibits the possibility. To be brutal, a human being has at least to come into physical contact with an animal, whereas in factory farming there is no meaningful relationship between human and beast at all. Animals are not treated as individual creatures with individual characters and needs; instead, they are − to quote the Ministry of Agriculture − a biomass, reduced to units in a production line for converting low-priced feed to high-priced animal flesh. The farmer no longer works directly with the stock, but is rather a machine operator, pressing buttons to ensure that light patterns, heat and feed systems are running efficiently. For instance, the only times that broiler chicken owners are likely to touch their birds are when they remove the dead during routine inspection or when they pack the fattened chicken off to the slaughterhouse.

The violence of factory farming is more than violence against animals. It is violence against life. Animals in modern intensive units do not suffer because we are sadistic towards them; they suffer because our lack of responsiveness has reached the point where we no longer recognize the life or individuality in them. They are simply walking lumps of food. D.H. Lawrence, considering humanity's vital relation to 'all things', writes of a white cock on his ranch in New Mexico:

> And as the white cock calls in the doorway, who calls? Merely a barnyard rooster worth a dollar and a half. But listen! Under the old dawns of creation the Holy Ghost, the Mediator, shouts aloud in the twilight. And every time I hear him, a fountain of vitality gushes up in my body. It is life.[1]

It would be foolish to suggest that this recognition of the otherness of animal life is all that we need to consider. Farmers will justifiably argue that if they are to keep animals for food, then they have to make profits and that Lawrence's — for want of a better word — poetic apprehension of life is largely incompatible with their work. Nevertheless, the question is still worth asking: how can we reconcile an appreciation of the mystery of all individual life with the squalor of battery cages? And what does it say about our civilization that we have allowed economic factors to dominate to such an extent that many people would feel inclined to laugh at Lawrence's 'soulful' apprehension of poultry. To us, the chicken is even less than 'a barnyard rooster worth a dollar and a half'. So much so, that descriptions echoing the following sentiments are not uncommon:

> The modern layer is, after all, only a very efficient converting machine, changing the raw material — feedstuffs — into the finished product — the egg — less, of course, maintenance requirements.[2]

The comparison between these two passages speaks for itself. When people present the argument that we should care about human misery more than animal suffering they are exposing a falsity, because the two are inseparable. The human attitude to living creatures exemplified by factory farming inevitably finds its parallel in our level of responsiveness to our own species. A genuine concern for life should extend to all living creatures.

## Hooked on violence

Once we adopt systems of keeping animals in conditions as unnatural as battery cages or sow stalls, we embark upon a path that leads, inevitably, to ever-escalating violence. The problem is that when animals are reared in environments wholly inconsistent with their needs, they do not passively accept their lot. Nature rebels.

Take the case of battery hens. In a crowded cage, standing on wire floors, birds cannot fulfil their strong urge to peck the ground for food. Consequently, another expression has to be found for that particular instinct. In the barren environment of cages, the only possible outlets are other birds. Therefore, the pecking instinct may well be redirected towards cage-mates. Scientists call this 'displacement behaviour' and it can result in considerable damage or even death through cannibalism to the bird that happens to be at the bottom of the pecking order.

The rational answer would be to accept this perversity by the hens as a sure indication that living conditions are unsuitable. Unfortunately, however, our current ethos towards animals leads in precisely the opposite direction. Debeaking to minimize damage caused by feather-pecking, antibiotics in feed to reduce stress, research on light patterns to induce docility without adversely affecting production, and more research on genetics in an attempt to breed aggression-free stock. Violence leads to further violence.

In his book *Bring Me My Bow*, John Seymour demonstrates superbly the way in which the same pattern affects pig farming:

> A pig is an animal evolved by natural selection to live on the ground, to suffer extremes of heat and cold, to search for its food with its nose and to root in the ground. As it does the latter it eats a good deal of earth. The sow is furnished with an elaborate chain of instincts which come into play when she is farrowing. Days before the event she starts searching for a place to build a nest, she carries straw about in her mouth from one place to another, finally she makes an elaborate nest and has her litter. She then suckles her piglets — and defends them if necessary with great ferocity — until they naturally wean themselves at the age of about 10 weeks.

Now inorganically-minded farmers started by taking the sow off the earth, keeping her on concrete, and giving her straw to lie on. It made their work easier. Her chain of instinct was upset by this confinement and she became clumsy and often lay on her pigs. The inorganic answer − to remove the straw and fit a farrowing rail. She became even more deprived and disturbed, her chain of instinct was even more upset, and she began to eat the piglets. Inorganic answer − put her in a farrowing crate where she could not turn round and could only with difficulty just stand up in one position and lay down. Then lure the piglets away from their mother with an infra-red light. Apart from the manifest cruelty of this (but agribusiness has never allowed itself to be deflected by considerations of humanity) it was found that the little semi-orphans became horribly subject to pulmonary complaints (anaemia had been cured by routine injections of iron). Inorganic answer − inject them with this and that, lace their food with antibiotics and heavy metals, keep them at a constant temperature and finally − the crowning obscenity perhaps of twentieth century 'agriculture', the practising of embryotomy: cutting the living piglets out of the womb of their dead mother in aseptic conditions so as to establish what is known, in the jargon, as a 'minimal disease herd'. And where can we go from there?[3]

Common sense should have told us from the beginning that it is unintelligent and insensitive to keep pigs − animals whose strongest instinct is to root in the ground − permanently confined in a narrow stall of concrete. Yet obvious symptoms of physical damage caused by 'inorganic thinking' have been treated only as problems to be overcome by human ingenuity. To give another example, in this extract from a report published by the Pig Veterinary Society, Mr G. Wells is discussing skin disorders found in baby piglets attributable to floor surfaces. His language is a little technical, but revealing:

Penny, Edwards and Mulley (1971) described local necrosis of the skin of suckling pigs, and from their observations and those of previous communications, concluded that the lesions were mainly due to trauma from concrete floors. Sites at which lesions were recorded included body, skin, coronets, ears, elbows, face, feet, fetlocks, hocks, knees, rump, sternum, tail, teats and vulva. Necrotic lesions of limbs developed rapidly, within a few hours of birth. Small abrasions became blackish-brown areas of dry gangrene, with subsequent scab formation and peeling by five weeks of age. Lesions were invariably bilateral and in order of decreasing incidence observed on the knee, fetlock, hock, elbow and coronet, with lesions on the chin, sternum and rump occurring less frequently than lesions on the limbs. Bruising of the feet at the sole/heel junction, leading sometimes to necrotic lesions was recorded in piglets less than 24 hours old.[4]

Is there any part of the piglets not suffering from sores or other injuries? Yet predictably, the response to such problems is normally more violence. Probably 'minor' injuries are ignored because they have no adverse affect upon mortality rates. Alternatively, more money is ploughed into research on modifying or finding new types of floors or applying new kinds of routine medication.

So far, our argument against violence in agriculture has dwelt only upon physical symptoms. Yet more intense suffering is probably caused by psychological stress. In Holland, Professor van Putten has undertaken revealing research[5] comparing the behaviour of piglets reared with their mothers in straw-yards, to litters weaned early and placed in flat-deck battery houses on a floor of perforated metal. The respective groups were filmed and observed 24 hours a day over a period of several weeks.

The results show that piglets brought up with the sow fulfil certain behaviour instincts. Unweaned piglets spend a considerable time sucking their mother's udder − up to 15 minutes every hour. Professor van Putten points out that this sucking is not simply answering nutritional needs, because the different sound and rhythm of the sow's grunting suggests that the piglet is only drinking for approximately one of those 15 minutes. Researchers conclude that this behaviour must also be satisfying a need for comfort, derived from massaging the udder. The piglets on straw also spent much of their time exploring by testing objects with their snout and displaying general interest in their environment.

Basically the difference in the battery cage was that there was no mother and nothing of interest in the cage. Lack of stimuli caused the piglets to display several abnormalities, such as sitting for prolonged periods in a dog-like position hardly ever adopted by those animals kept in a more stimulating environment. Professor van Putten explains how this behaviour must be caused by both the boredom and discomfort of standing on wire-mesh floors. Piglets were also found to be nibbling penmates or the cage structure because there was no outlet for their inquisitiveness. Finally, since there was no sow's udder for them to suck, they redirected this urge towards penmates or lifeless objects.

An indication of the way that lack of stimuli may retard development as well as causing boredom and frustration (as with human children) is that by the time that the piglets running with the sow were 7 weeks old, no incident of them sucking their penmates was recorded. At the same age, piglets in the battery cage could still be seen frequently sucking their cage-mates on the ear, navel, penis, vulva or tail. In other words, the research intimates that the combined effects of battery cages and maternal deprivation, restrict piglets' normal patterns of psychological growth. Yet despite this, Professor van Putten found little difference in physical growth rates. Indeed, the caged piglets reared artificially on milk substitute put on weight slightly quicker than those running with the sow.

This research demonstrates the falsity of the argument that 'animals wouldn't put on weight if they weren't happy'. Clearly, enormous psychological stress can be endured without any adverse effects upon productivity. It is as ridiculous to claim that growth rates alone are a reliable measure of overall health as it is to suggest that physical stature can give an accurate guide to human well-being.

There is a definite parallel between the mechanistic attitude to farm animals described hitherto and the search for profits that has prompted their adoption. For the profit motive utilizes the same principles, leading to a similar escalation of violence. It works in the following way. In the beginning somebody has the idea that if he puts one hen in a cage in an environmentally controlled battery house, he can stack three or four cages on top of each other, and control heat and light patterns to ensure that he can keep more hens and produce more eggs more cheaply than under extensive conditions. His methods prove profitable, so he expands his business. Soon he is selling so many cheap eggs that the smaller profits enjoyed by the extensive farmer begin to disappear. This leaves the extensive producer with two choices: either to sell his business to the battery producer or to copy his methods. As a result everybody soon has one bird in a cage and nobody makes any extra profit. Then someone else comes along and discovers that you can put two birds in a cage. His profits roll in for a while, until, of course, everybody copies again, and so on. Eventually a stage is reached like today's conditions, with five birds in a cage 18 inches by 20 inches — and egg producers still complaining about lack of profits and unfair competition from overseas.

The history of John Eastwood highlights this process. In 1964 he set himself the target of supplying one-third of the nation's eggs, a target he never reached despite becoming Britain's largest producer. In 1978, this principal figure in the development of the battery egg business sold his empire of 7½ million hens. He did so stating that 'so many had copied his methods' that profits had been drastically reduced,[6] despite all the 'advances' introduced into egg production over the years (i.e. less space per bird, genetic developments, etc.).

Always, in the greater struggle for profits, it is the animal that suffers; and the more narrow the profit margins become, so the more desperate become the measures employed. For instance, one broiler chicken farmer, rearing birds on contract to a larger concern, told me frankly that he is being pressurized into adopting stocking densities which he knows to be detrimental to the physical welfare of the chickens. Stock are being crammed into his broiler house at a rate that ensures that a percentage of birds are trampled upon and either die or suffer dislocated or broken backs, legs or wings. This overcrowding is encouraged because, according to profitability graphs, the number of birds killed or 'downgraded' because of injury are worth less money than the additional profits which are made by rearing extra numbers in the broiler shed. We have allowed 'efficiency' — where technical feasibility is the only criterion considered in production method — and materialism — where profit dominates totally — to take control of our farming. Since both philosophies ignore any living response to animals, it is inevitable that they result in ever-increasing violence. It is no wonder that the lives of our farm animals are now controlled by the same principles employed in any industrial operation. In *Small is Beautiful*, E.F. Schumacher highlights the limitation of such an attitude:

> If I have a car, a man-made thing, I might quite legitimately argue that the best way to use it is never to bother about maintenance and simply run it to ruin. I may indeed have calculated that this is the most economical method of use. If the calculation is correct, nobody can criticize me for acting accordingly, for there is nothing sacred about a man-made thing like a car. But if I have an animal − be it only a calf or a hen − a living creature, am I allowed to treat it as nothing but a utility? Am I allowed to run it to ruin?[7]

Literally, our failure to distinguish between 'a man-made thing' and 'a living sensitive creature' is an inability to separate life from death.

## Where do we go from here?

When we examine the overcrowding in factory farms, some small comfort may be derived from the recognition that as far as stocking densities are concerned, it appears physically impossible to cram many more animals into existing cages, crates or sheds. Unfortunately, however, this does not necessarily mean the end of battery systems. On the contrary, whilst present-day attitudes prevail, it merely suggests that more sophisticated ways of exploitation will be invented.

One area of possible 'improvement' is in greater control over environment. Flooring, temperature and light patterns are varied and tested in an attempt to improve performance; plastic, mesh, concrete, metal and slats are constantly researched in the search for better flooring. Other research is more bizarre: broiler chickens have been fitted with blinkers and even contact lenses in attempts to reduce aggression.

Diet offers another opportunity to cut costs. 'Sawdust, sand and china clay'[8] are used as 'fillers' in some pig feeds. Recycled dung is a relatively common ingredient and concrete dust has been tried in cattle diets. Inevitably, we tend to overlook some of the smaller deprivations involved in factory farming, but it is worth recording that animals enjoy a varied diet, just like humans. For instance, pigs have twice as many taste-buds as we do, yet all they receive under intensive methods is the same pelleted food day after day.

For adding to animal feeds we can expect pharmaceutical companies to increase their range of 'animal health products'. Although government legislation does offer some protection against proliferation of drugs, the concerns which dominate the pharmaceutical industry sometimes succeed in lowering standards. For example, until 1980, tylosin was considered a 'therapeutic substance' and was available only on prescription; now it is available on free-sale and widely promoted in farming magazine advertisements. Protestors against this change included the British Veterinary Association, who argued that the decision undermined the whole concept of Britain's attempt to control the availability of therapeutic medicines in livestock farming.

Unless the principle of factory farming is opposed emphatically, it will spread to other animals. Ducks, geese, partridges and even quail have all been intensively reared in recent years. The rabbit trade now involves over a million animals per annum.[9] In research, a method of inducing multiple births in ewes by utilizing fertility drugs is well established. The extra lambs that the ewe is unable to rear from her own milk can then be raised on an artificial diet, possibly in cages.[10]

The most disturbing of all potential areas of progress is in the work undertaken by geneticists. In the 1950s it took 10 weeks to fatten 3-5lb chickens; now it takes just over 7 weeks. In five years' time, scientists predict 'significant improvements' with killing ages reduced to 42-44 days.[11] Featherless chickens have been the aim of researchers throughout the world (suitable to all climates), whilst the dwarf 'mini-mother' is becoming well established amongst breeding stock for chicken production.

Progress in pig farming also owes much to geneticists. 'The main scientific advances have come from genetic improvements',[12] Dr Colin Whittmore, head of animal production and development at East of Scotland College of Agriculture, told a recent conference. He added that 'in future the industry can hope to see a major thrust in productivity from the science of reproductive physiology.[13]

A more bizarre example of the genetic mind at work is Dr John King of the Animal Breeding Organization. He envisages the insertion of genes to make pigs grow wool. As pigs breed more quickly and produce larger litters than sheep, this would create the possibility of both more wool and more meat.[14] Another centre for genetic developments in this country is the notorious research centre at Babraham, near Cambridge. Animals with instruments embedded in their skulls and sides, and goats' udders transplanted to their necks are amongst the unexplained activities at Babraham.[15]

The vision behind these enterprises is that eventually scientists will be able to produce living creatures that are not only super-productive and super-resistant to stress, but also differ from their ancestors so totally that they will 'belong' to a factory farm and be completely satisfied by a barren environment. Quite literally, the aim is to perfect food-producing machines by eliminating all the qualities that make animals living creatures.

There is one other important area where scientists may be able to increase productivity. Namely, in the earlier separation of mother from young. For example, piglets are now commonly weaned under 3 weeks old, and at the Rowett Research Institute experiments into weaning at birth are underway. *Pig Farming* magazine describes the work as follows:

> In the new unit, an automated system is being developed to remove piglets — identified by an electric grid — on a slow-moving rubber conveyor belt. This takes the piglets through a trap door in the wall, and into the adjoining rearing room. Low-intensity, ultra-violet light kills any bacteria remaining in the trap. Elaborate precautions are taken to prevent dams passing on 'bugs' to their offspring — down to polythene sheeting over the sows to ensure that newly born piglets do not even breathe the same air as their mother. Some of the piglets are then reared in kitchen waste-bins turned on to their side and adapted into incubators with the help of ventilators and perspex covers. After two weeks they are transferred to conventional battery cages.[16]

Notice again how violence to animals is self-perpetuating. Apart from the horrific ingenuity of the research itself one of the most revealing features of this quotation is that battery cages for piglets — a recent phenomenon — can be thought of as 'conventional'. The extremes of one decade quickly become the norm of the next, to be replaced by an even greater injustice. Evidently, there is no prospect of reversing current trends until it is acknowledged that animals are primarily sensitive creatures with individual needs rather than products on a plate, statistics on a graph, tools for research or cogs in a machine for converting grain to flesh.

Some commercial enterprises have gone one step further than weaning at birth. The practice of pig embryotomy is gaining in popularity. The aim is to obtain completely disease-free piglets for breeding purposes by slaughtering the sow shortly before she is about to farrow, removing the piglets and then racing them to the farm in sterile containers. Because of the considerable expense involved, this method is only employed upon 'best quality' breeding stock.

With some justification, pessimists may argue that mankind has always displayed the same callous attitudes to animals, the only difference now being that we have the capacity to inflict suffering on such a massive scale. Yet this does not alter the validity of the case made here. Just as the potentially horrendous consequences of nuclear war demand that mankind exercise increasing control over his warlike impulses, so, on a less dramatic scale, the degree and scale of violence that technological advances allow us to inflict upon animals, makes it essential that we question deeply our attitudes towards other creatures. The third part of this book examines ways in which we can work towards the ideal of non-violent farming, but before that part two takes a closer look at the main arguments used to defend current practices.

Part two

# ...And a few tall stories

# Introduction

In this section we shall be asking who benefits from factory farming. At different times it is argued that animals benefit; that consumers benefit; that it is helping to feed the starving in poorer countries; that it is better for agricultural workers; and that it is the only possible way of producing adequate amounts of food. The standpoint of this book is that the section of the community which actually benefits from battery farming are the people who make financial profits out of it. Primarily, this means the large multinational concerns, who, along with their allies in the Stock Exchange, increasingly dominate the direction which farming takes.

# 6. Myth one: scientific objectivity

The defences of factory farming are extremely predictable. Opponents are accused of ignorant emotionalism, and 'expert' scientific evidence is quoted alongside economic justifications to prove the error of amateur opinions. Every time it finds itself threatened, the farming industry responds with some variation upon the theme, 'we need facts − not emotion'.[1] Agriculture, we are told, needs 'objective assessment of the significance of stress upon farm animals'.[2] 'It is futile to attribute human reactions, human fears and human interpretations to the animal mind.'[3] 'Sense or sentiment',[4] 'emotion versus reason'.[5] The examples are numerous. The Ministry of Agriculture take the same line, assuring protestors that the ministry makes assessments based upon 'scientific training' and 'clinical observation',[6] qualities which dispel any possible fears about cruelty. The president of the National Farmers' Union, Sir Richard Butler, introduces his own variation on the theme, stating that the debate over animal welfare has 'reached the lowest level of emotion'.[7]

In all these defences, fact, objectivity and truth are associated with 'scientific training', and emotion is linked to a sort of neurotic ignorance. At best, protestors are presented as well meaning, but lacking the authoritative 'expert' knowledge necessary to make judgements. A document which highlights this tactic magnificently is *The Welfare of Livestock*, produced by the Farm Animal Welfare Advisory Committee. FAWAC was a committee elected to serve as the Minister of Agriculture's guiding light on animal welfare. Its members were divided so irreconcilably between those who genuinely wanted to see change and those who had vested interests in existing practices, that in their report they were forced to offer their findings under two separate headings. What we shall call the welfare group, called their approach 'ethical'; the others labelled themselves 'scientific'.

Under these two headings all the major questions raised by factory farming were discussed. For example, should animals have room to turn around? Not suprisingly, the ethical group felt that the ministry should 'discourage all husbandry systems which deny animals freedom to move around'.[8] The scientific group responded with this:

> There is no evidence that the inability to turn around *per se* causes stress in animals. Prolonged tethering has been practised for many years in the North without discernible ill effects. It is necessary, however, to be sure that tethered animals have sufficient freedom to groom themselves and to lie down naturally and without difficulty. The argument that all animals have a fundamental right to be able to turn around is essentially anthropomorphic. It is not just a question of giving the benefit of the doubt to the animal because scientifically speaking there is no doubt involved. The ethical argument must be regarded as weak in the light of available knowledge to the contrary, and there is no justification for revising the code to permit animals to turn around.[9]

This is typical of the 'scientific' argument put forward throughout the FAWAC booklet, according to which, there is no reason why animals should not be kept in dim lighting, or on concrete floors; calves have no need of bedding; permanent tethering is perfectly acceptable and debeaking of hens 'causes very little trouble to the birds'. Although it was published back in 1970, *The Welfare of Livestock* remains representative of the 'scientific' grounds on which factory farming methods (and many other questionable practices in modern life) are justified by authority. Indeed, this association between science and fact is now so uncritically accepted by most sections of the community that even those people whose objections are based upon moral grounds find themselves scrabbling excitedly for scientific papers which support their views, in the sure knowledge that they will add plausibility to what is otherwise dismissed as mere 'emotion'.

For example, Dr Marion Dawkins of the Animal Behaviour Research Group at the Department of Zoology in Oxford, conducted a number of experiments with hens. She undertook a series of 'preference tests' in which two groups of hens — one kept in battery cages and one on free-range — were offered a choice of environments.[10]

At first, all the birds stuck to the system to which they were accustomed, but gradually they became inquisitive and started to investigate the alternative, until both groups eventually plumped for free-range. In a second trial, a choice between free-range alone or battery cages with companions was set up. Nine out of 10 chose the former, the remaining bird being affected by seeking a place to lay an egg. Finally, when the alternatives were either free-range without food or a cage with access to food, only 3 out of 10 decided to go into the cage. In conclusion, Dr Dawkins's research indicates clearly that hens prefer free-range conditions, but does it actually tell us anything that common sense did not tell us before? The tests merely demonstrate what most 'non-experts' would conclude for themselves without needing data to support their views. Whilst it is right that we should base our judgements about factory farming, or any other matter, upon fact, the assumption that science deals exclusively with fact and that emotion invariably excludes it, is a dangerous nonsense.

Take anthropomorphism for instance — that is, attributing human forms and personality to animals. When taken to extremes, such as attributing human moral values or appreciation of beauty to animals, it can obviously become as ridiculous as the scientific experts would have us believe. Yet on the other hand, many of what we like to think of as human characteristics clearly do exist in farm animals. Observation of a group of calves or young pigs in a field cannot fail to show behaviour comparable to that of young children — boundless energy one moment, fast asleep the next, a sense of fun and adventure, curiosity in what goes on around them, mischievousness, a close bond with their parents, and enjoyment in the companionship of their own species. None of these qualities can be proved by scientific experiments, but they are still facts. Whilst anthropomorphism admittedly cannot give us an exact assessment of the needs and experiences of animals, it is, nevertheless, basically the best method available to us. As we are human beings and not pigs, cows or chickens, we have only human feelings and thoughts on which to base our decisions. To try and exclude these or to imagine that through some completely objective scientific discovery we can produce 'conclusive evidence', is to deny all the qualities by which we create any worthwhile human values. In a real sense it is to become subhuman.

If the reader remains unconvinced that anthropomorphism is the only method available to us, it is worth looking at the theories put forward by advocates of factory farming. For the crowning irony is that although they dismiss anthropomorphism in one breath, in the next they themselves invariably resort to the same principles. Here is part of a report in *Farmers' Guardian* of a speech in defence of the battery cage by Professor Oliver King, head of the Animal Husbandry Department of Liverpool University, ex-president of the Royal College of Veterinary Surgeons, and a member of the government's latest advisory committee on animal welfare, the Farm Animal Welfare Council (FAWC).

> Pecking order also had no role in the battery context. Its value lay in the wild in times of food shortage... Nesting behaviour was not important in the cage situation. Body care, such as dust bathing to give relief from parasites, was not needed as birds in batteries were comparatively free of parasites, and in any case the tendency to move high up, or perch at rest was a protective measure against predators which were not a threat to battery-housed hens. 'Waltzing' behaviour was related to breeding, therefore unimportant in the cage situation said Prof. King.[11]

This takes a common defence of factory farming — 'if they are born in cages they never know any different' — to new and bizarre lengths. According to this report, Professor King is suggesting that the total absence of opportunity for natural behaviour in battery cages is their chief merit, since a barren environment renders inherited instincts redundant. Yet how are the hens supposed to realize that they have no need of perches when there are no predators about? They would be able to do so only if they were capable of reaching some kind of rational judgement which enabled them to cast off patterns of behaviour established over centuries. They would need human logic.

Wherever you look for defences of factory farming you will find anthropomorphism. Even the simple theory that animals are better off in cages and crates than outside in cold weather is a potent example of human values being applied to animal life. Indeed, it must be repeated that there is no choice other than to base our assessments upon human feelings, since we *are* humans and not other animals. What we can and must ensure, however, is that when we do make judgements we make them as intelligently as we possibly can, derived from sympathetic interest and close observation of how animals actually behave, rather than through preconditioned theories. Of the two ideas quoted so far, the one attributed to Professor King falls outside this category. It suggests a level of consciousness which hens show no sign of possessing; and the argument that hens are better off in cages than outside in mud and rain is equally unconvincing. Although based on a grain of truth in that hens, like humans, do often appear miserable in wet and cold weather, it conveniently ignores the fact that on well-managed farms, free-range birds are also provided with adequate shelter. Normally, they *choose* to go outside during bad weather, even though they will remain there for only a short period before returning to the hen house.

Often, it is not only anthropomorphism that scientists resort to in order to 'prove' their point. Frequently they accuse supporters of animal rights of being 'sentimental' about animals, yet, they themselves are ready to resort to blatant sentimentality in order to lend weight to their viewpoint. For example, at Cornell University, experiments in raising lambs in battery cages have been conducted. In praise of this work, one member of the Cornell staff wrote:

> Its amazing how fast a pair of lambs adapt to the cages.
> They feel very comfortable in them. They have their
> 'friends' with them, so they aren't lonely, and they seem to
> regard the cage as home — they feel safe.[12]

Friendship, comfort, companionship, security and safety — all highly valued aspects of human life — are introduced here to create a reassuring image of the researcher as benevolent guardian of the animals under his care. Others might interpret these words as nothing more than a sentimental rationalization of taking young creatures, traditionally associated with spring and new life, out of their natural environment and robbing them of both their mothers and the possibility of fulfilling their grazing instincts. Certainly, it is interesting that another member of the Cornell staff advocates the high potential of cage rearing only on the grounds that it produces 'a pretty nice cash-flow situation'.[13] Sceptics might argue that the latter statement reaches nearer to the truth about the driving force behind research into battery lamb production.

In chapter 5 we discussed work undertaken at the Rowett Research Institute into weaning piglets at birth and rearing them in converted kitchen bins. Answering widespread criticism, Sir Kenneth Blaxter, head of Rowett, made the following statement:

> The piglets when born are placed in incubators, to ensure that they all receive adequate food and warmth and are not subject to infection from the dung of the mother sow. The work is experimental. It is possible that some modification of the maternity ward and infant survival unit approach might be adopted in commerce in future, but, at present the objective is to see whether mortality and morbidity can, in fact, be reduced... The incubators themselves are indeed plastic waste-bins. They are fitted with perspex fronts and rears so that the piglets can see one another and are supplied with warm, bacterially filtered air. The merit of the plastic bin is that it is much kinder to the piglets than steel and is readily sterilized before use.[14]

Superficially, Sir Kenneth Blaxter seems to present a laudable aim: 'to see whether mortality and morbidity can, in fact be reduced'. When we look closely, however, almost every phrase represents an attempt to use sentimentality in order to glorify ruthless exploitation. As another member of the Rowett staff revealingly stated, the goal is 'to get more out of the sow'. The nature of the research actually dictates that the animal is regarded only as a machine for producing food.

The comparison to a 'maternity ward and infant survival unit' is introduced only to suggest that the research scientist is a figure fighting for the preservation of life, saving piglets in the same way that doctors save human children. But why is the scientist interested in saving piglets' lives? Certainly not to return them to their mothers! Nor have the piglets been selected for treatment because they are in need of special medical care. The fact that young pigs develop far quicker than human children and by nature would be enthusiastically darting around with fellow creatures before their period in the incubator finishes, is also conveniently ignored. Also, Sir Kenneth points to another highly esteemed human virtue, cleanliness, in order to diminish the relationship between young and mother pigs. Early-weaned piglets, we are told are 'not subject to infection from the dung of the mother sow'. This implies that the bond between sow and piglet is both trivial and rather unclean. Yet in the wild, pigs live in a developed family group, are scrupulously clean and weaning is a slow process. Early weaning represents a traumatic period for young pigs. All of this is conveniently ignored and the hygienic, 'warm, bacterially filtered air' is offered as a pleasant-sounding substitute. One final point: the assertion that plastic floors are 'kinder' than steel, implies that steel and plastic are the only choices. Have they never heard of the earth or at least straw?

To associate 'kindness' with the rearing of pigs in converted plastic bins is to use an emotionally charged word where it has no meaningful place. On the other hand, to associate a sense of fun and adventure with young animals is to base one's response upon observable phenomena. The former is outright sentimentality — what D.H. Lawrence called 'the working off on yourself of feelings you haven't really got' — the latter is emotion based upon fact.

'Ignorance' is another insult that 'experts' tend to use in order to castigate animal rights campaigners. Yet it would be difficult to imagine a clearer example of ignorance about animals than that shown by researchers at the partly government-funded Animal Breeding Research Organization, when they subjected different breeds of new-born lambs to simulated adverse weather conditions in wind tunnels. From their experiments, they concluded that lambs with heavy coats coped better with high winds, cold and wet, than those with light fleeces![15] Admittedly, research at the Scottish Farm Buildings Investigation Unit into aggressive behaviour amongst pigs at feeding time has more validity. Nevertheless, we are forced to question whether experiments as obvious as the following truly justify allocation of taxpayers' money:

> Although Mike Baxter still has to evaluate a few of his results recorded on video, he has already found that varying the period between feeds influences the time that pigs remain at the food trough. For instance, pigs fed at six-hourly intervals feed for about 20 minutes, whereas when they are fed every 24 hours they actually stay at the feed trough for an hour at a time.[16]

What of the popular concept that science can somehow produce 'conclusive proof'? In August 1979, the journal *Pig Farming* announced that the Animal Breeding Research Organization had published a report of tests carried out into the weaning of piglets. Contrary to all modern trends, ABRO had concluded that it would be economically advantageous to leave piglets with their mother for several weeks before weaning. *Pig Farming* heralded this as 'a bombshell'. The same week *Meat Traders' Journal* reported a speech by Dr Richard Broade of the National Institute of Research in Dairying at Reading. Apparently, Dr Broade had spoken proudly of what he considered the doubled efficiency of pig farming in the UK over the last 50 years. He added that there was still 'considerable room for further progress'. Amongst areas of progress anticipated was the artificial weaning of piglets at a few days old or perhaps at birth. Two reports from two scientists within two days, offering totally irreconcilable conclusions; and both of them suggesting that the government's own pig 'experts', who only a month before had advocated 14 days as the optimum time for weaning piglets, were inaccurate.

The results which any researchers achieve are inevitably affected by the preconceptions with which they begin. For instance, someone whose response to animal life lies somewhere in the tradition of the highly influential eighteenth-century philosopher René Descartes, who believed that animals only ever react mechanically and therefore are incapable of feelings, would differ fundamentally from another who perhaps shares some of Gandhi's active compassion for all life. Differences will manifest themselves at all levels — in the nature of the experiments themselves, the level of intuitive awareness, responsiveness to suffering and stress in the animals observed, and subsequently in the results and their interpretation. A researcher who is only aware of growth and mortality rates will miss symptoms of suffering that a more sympathetic individual would notice immediately.

Regrettably, there do seem to be numerous agricultural scientists who fall into the former category. Indeed, all those who accept factory farming's popular defence — that animals would not put on weight if they were not happy — are allying themselves unequivocally with the Cartesian principle. Apart from ignoring the way that carefully regulated high-protein food, genetic engineering and routine use of drugs can ensure that an animal under stress continues to be productive, it throws in the concept of happiness to disguise a purely mechanistic principle — another example of sentimentality. Once we accept growth or reproduction rates, food conversion graphs, blood chemistry counts or other statistical information as the sole measure of animal welfare, we fall prey to the same reductive evaluation of life that led the philosopher and his followers to conclude that an animal squealing with pain is simply the equivalent of noise from a compressed spring that had been released. Is it essentially any different to argue that animals who fatten up quickly or reproduce are automatically content?

There remains a great deal to learn about animals and their needs and it would be as ridiculous to argue that science has no part in these explorations as it would be to claim that arrogance, ignorance, stupidity and sentimentality are labels to be pinned upon all agricultural scientists. It is simply the respect afforded unquestioningly to the concept of 'scientific truth' that needs to be opposed. Science and technology have proved themselves capable of developing methods of farming where animals remain productive when denied movement and exercise. But it does not automatically follow that the right of animals to turn around can be dismissed as 'essentially anthropomorphic'. The former is a technical problem which scientists have proved themselves capable of conquering; the rights of animals are unquantifiable and must be assessed according to different criteria. Essentially, it is an ethical question.

Unfortunately, in animal welfare, as in so many areas of our society, we have taken technical proficiency for something greater than it actually is. The dangers of such an ethos are exposed by E.F. Schumacher:

> Science and engineering produce know-how; but know-how is nothing by itself; it is a means without an end, a mere potentiality, an unfinished sentence. Know-how is no more a culture than a piano is music... There is no doubt also about the need to transmit know-how but this must take second place, for it is obviously somewhat foolhardy to put great powers into the hands of people without making sure that they have a reasonable idea of what to do with them. At present, there can be no doubt that the whole of mankind is in mortal danger, not because we are short of scientific and

technological know-how, but because we tend to use it destructively, without wisdom.[17]

Surely the treatment of animals in our laboratories and on our farms represents one of the most blatant examples available of 'know-how' used 'destructively, without wisdom'.

It is no coincidence that in farm animal welfare it is those with vested interests who most frequently resort to this need for 'scientific fact — not emotion'. Science has become their tool, providing both the technical requirements to operate factory farms and at the same time justification of the methods, based on society's almost religious acceptance of the authority of science. This state of affairs suits both researchers and 'the establishment', be it governments, or multinational companies. For example, consider this statement in defence of the battery cage for laying hens, made by Mr H.A. Elson, National Specialist in poultry environment for the Ministry of Agriculture's Advisory Department (ADAS).

> Essential behavioural and welfare needs of poultry have not yet been fully defined, so no one can produce conclusive evidence of the specific needs of the bird in respect of space requirements, feed troughs, allowance, suitability of a particular system. All that is possible at present, therefore, is that sound management should be practised within guidelines such as the Codes of Practice.[18]

Poultry cannot talk and humans cannot transform themselves into poultry, so how can we possibly have the 'conclusive evidence' that Mr Elson is seeking? If we wait for the day when scientists can minutely measure 'specific needs' of hens in the terms Mr Elson is suggesting, we will wait forever. Literally. Perhaps this is the idea? As long as the need for and the possibility of conclusive proof about animal behaviour is presented as a question awaiting an unequivocal answer, then the researcher assures himself a permanent position of high esteem and the vested interests are protected by a perfect excuse for defending existing practices. They can avoid confronting what is fundamentally a moral question by arguing that scientific discovery will transfer it into a purely technical one. But it never will.

To end this chapter on a more positive note, let us look briefly at some of the research carried out with pigs by Professor van Putten of Holland, whose work on the deprivation suffered by battery piglets was examined in chapter 5. Both his work and more particularly the responsiveness to animal life behind the research, offers an enlightening comparison to some of the statements we have so far discussed. Like any other research scientist he is thorough in his analysis and his work is full of the conventional graphs and statistics detailing his findings about pigs. Yet there is much more. Unlike many of his contemporaries, his interest in the animals under his dominion demands that they are more than a set of figures to support a scientific or economic theory. He is never dominated by a sense of his own or his work's overriding importance and is always aware that he is working with sensitive creatures, What is more, he is not afraid to say so in terms which would be likely to promote ridicule had they been made by an 'emotional' non-expert.

> Anyone coming close to a pig, say for better understanding of its own needs, will discover that he is not dealing with a dummy, but with an alert animal with its own dignity and its own needs. Accepting responsibility for farm animals' welfare means more than providing food, water and shelter.[19]

In other papers, he draws attention to the importance of comfort to pigs. He illustrates how they will spend considerable periods grooming, lying in wet places to lose body heat, and wallowing in mud to stimulate skin and hair care. They will bathe on hot days and are excellent swimmers. They will scratch their heads and neck to relieve itches or rub against low branches of trees. Yawning, stretching, shaking, lying close together and tucking in straw to make a comfortable bed are amongst the varied habits that he has noted in unrestrained pigs. These activities lead him to the conclusion that grooming is vital to pig welfare and that if we keep them in any kind of intensive systems we should supply bristles for them to groom on and showers to allow bathing![20] Unafraid to use anthropomorphic comparisons, he compares an ungroomed pig to a man unwashed and unshaven. Professor van Putten's interesting observations are living proof of the conclusion he makes to one of his papers: 'domestic pigs are by no means degenerated into walking sausages'.[21] This may seem an obvious statement, but it is one that modern agricultural thinking often totally ignores.

Finally, some ideas about pigs from a political figure-cum-farmer who lived at the turn of the nineteenth century, William Cobbett:

> In keeping hogs in a growing stage we must never forget their lodging! A few boards, flung carelessly over a couple of rails and no litter beneath, is not the sort of bed for a hog. A place of suitable size, large rather than small..., a floor constantly well bedded with leaves of trees, dry, and what a hog deserves, plenty of clean straw. When I make up my hogs' lodging place for winter I look well at it and consider whether, upon a pinch, I could, for once in a way, make shift to lodge in it myself. If I shiver at the thought, the place is not good enough for them. It is not in the nature of a hog to sleep in the cold.[22]

> I had a sow that had some pigs running about with her in April last. There was a place open to her on each side of the barn... one evening her pigs had gone to bed on the east side. She was out eating till it began to grow dusk... I saw her go into her pigs and was surprised to see her come out again; and therefore, looked a little to see what she was after. There was a high heap of dung in the front of the barn to the south. She walked to the top of it, raised her nose, turned it very slowly two or three times, from the northeast to the northwest and back again, and at last it settled at about southeast for a little bit. She then came back, marched away very hastily to her pigs, roused them up in a great bustle, and away she trampled with them at her heels to the place on the west side of the barn... Was this *instinctive* or was it a *reasoning* proceeding? At any rate let us not treat such animals as if they were stocks and stones.[23]

Cobbett was not an agricultural scientist. But he lived and worked with animals and in these two passages we see something of the same spirit found in the work of Professor van Putten. In particular, an unsentimental interest in animals, thoughtful concern about their responses and general behaviour as when he ponders whether the sow moving her piglets was instinctive or reasoned, and outrage against any system that fails to recognize vitality and intelligence in pigs. Cobbett's 'let us not treat such animals as if they were stocks and stones' clearly derives from the same observations and sentiments as van Putten's 'domestic pigs are by no means degenerated into walking sausages'.

It is no coincidence that a nineteenth-century farmer working before modern animal science had been dreamt about, and a twentieth-century agricultural scientist enjoying all the new knowledge of many scientific developments, come to precisely the same conclusions. Furthermore, they use the same criteria for reaching those decisions, and display a similarly sympathetic awareness of the creatures they observe. Their findings exemplify what this chapter sets out to demonstrate. Namely, that there is an enormous amount of nonsense talked about 'scientific observation' enabling us to justify systems of livestock keeping that are simply unjustifiable. Cobbett and van Putten show us that however long mankind lives upon this planet he has only one true method of assessing problems involving living things. A scientist or non-scientist, if reasonably responsive, observant and interested in animals, will reach the conclusion that factory farming is indefensible. As to the 'scientific expert' myth, it is basically a deception designed to make profits for big business.

# 7. Myth two: public demand

How far is the development of livestock farming into a highly mechanized multimillion pound enterprise, in which 3,000 creatures are slaughtered in Britain every minute of every working day,[1] simply the result of the farming community answering consumer demand for massive quantities of animal protein? This is the question to be discussed in this chapter.

Factory farming systems were not developed by farmers. They are predominantly the result of expensive research carried out by agricultural scientists and financed by big business and government. In the past 30 years, multinational companies have taken over large shares of our animal farms, leaving the small producer with only limited control over his own livelihood. In particular, the poultry industry is dominated by a handful of 'giant' companies with the money-power and influence to manipulate all aspects of production. By 1981, eight firms provided some 63 per cent of the total UK output of broiler chickens; five firms provided 41 per cent of our egg supplies; and six were responsible for 70 per cent of the turkey trade.[2] Sometimes opponents of factory farming are accused of a lack of knowledge of farming. Yet a quick glance at the names monopolizing poultry production in the UK is sufficient to show that these allegations could more accurately be applied to those who control our farming (see table 7.1). To say the least, very few of them could be described as traditional farming enterprises! Big business domination does not end with the farm animals themselves. Unilever, Hillsdown and Cargill, together with Courtaulds, Union International and Bibby, also control about 40 per cent of total broiler and turkey feed sales and 20 per cent of laying hens' feed requirements.[3]

The consequences of only a few companies owning such large shares are enormous. Just as supermarkets were largely able to force

*Table 7.1* Estimated poultry and egg market shares, 1980

| Company | Broilers % | Turkeys % | Eggs % |
|---|---|---|---|
| Imperial Group* | 20 | 14 | 11 |
| Corgill | 7 | 9 | |
| Unilever | 4 | 9 | |
| Marshall | 9 | | |
| Courtaulds | 6 | | |
| Fitch Lorell | 6 | | |
| Union International | 6 | | |
| G.W. Padley | 5 | | |
| Bernard Matthews | | 21 | |
| Bibby | | 10 | |
| Swifts | | 7 | |
| Goldenlay | | | 15 |
| Dalgety | | | 5 |
| CWS | | | 5 |
| Stonegate | | | 5 |
| Remainder | 37 | 30 | 59 |
| Total UK market | 382 million birds | 23.3 million birds | 38.9 million cases (30 eggs per case) |

* In 1982, Imperial Group sold their poultry interests to Hillsdown Holdings.
Source: *Poultry World*, 19 November 1981

small shopkeepers out of business by their sheer capacity to lay out capital on an enormous scale, so the agribusiness world has used similar tactics to make life extraordinarily difficult for independent small farmers. With capital readily available out of the profits from other enterprises, multinationals are able to cut costs at all points of production. They can qualify for maximum discount by utilizing feedstuff raw materials in huge quantities; they can finance research at all levels to reduce production costs; set up huge hatcheries, feed mills, farms and slaughterhouses; employ the latest technological money-saving innovations; organize large-scale marketing and distribution facilities; and so on. Without actually owning the whole poultry industry, they have gained more than enough power to dictate the direction of poultry farming development.

The smallholder is left in an unfortunate position. Admittedly, there is now a growing market for the producer who refuses to conform to accepted factory farming policies and instead provides a better, more humanely produced non-battery product. Yet at the time when the takeover of the poultry industry was truly effected, the public were ignorant of both the involvement of big business and the consequences for animal welfare. Factory farming was well established before the majority of the public had any idea what went on inside battery farms. It took courage and considerable marketing ability for the small producer to maintain independence. For the majority, there appeared only three choices: to get out of farming; to be taken over by or work on contract to the large companies; or to join massive marketing co-operatives like Goldenlay,[4] and copy the methods employed by multinationals.

Looking at conditions inside factory farms, it would be easy to reach the false conclusion that all factory farmers must be evil men, obsessed by greed. No doubt a minority fit this description; most of them do not. It does not take evil men to operate evil systems. Some farmers are in factory farming solely for profit; others go along with it because it seems to them the only way of making a living out of a chosen trade. Without wishing to sentimentalize farmers, it is important to remember that in some ways many of them are also victims, as control over their livelihoods has been taken out of their hands to a large extent.

Although big business dominance is less complete in other areas of livestock production, it is nevertheless increasingly evident. Of the total amount of animal feed sold in this country – said to be worth some £1,300 million per annum – six companies account for 62 per cent.[5] BOCM Silcock, another part of the Unilever group, are by far the biggest company, supplying 21 per cent of the market. These are followed by Dalgety Spillers, Rank Hovis McDougall, Bibby and Nitrovit (part of the old Imperial group).[6]

Some of the same names also tend to appear at all other levels of meat production. For instance, Unilever own Walls Meat Co. and Mattesons, and are the biggest single producers of sausage meat in the country; Dalgety have a whole range of interests including slaughterhouses (Dalgety Buswells), meat companies (British Bacon Ltd) and suppliers of breeding stock (Pig Improvement Co.). In advertisements, Dalgety claim proudly that one in 12 breeding pigs comes from their stock. In all, 'a little over 6 per cent of producers account for more than half of Britain's production of pork and bacon'.[7]

Most of the big companies are also able to run their own research centres or else sponsor courses in university departments. By doing so, they put themselves in an unchallengeable position where they can influence the direction of agricultural research and ensure that it centres upon providing extra profits rather than humane conditions for animals.

From all this we can see that, whether or not factory farming is providing a public service, it is certainly not farmers who are dictating supply. Yet the question still remains: even if the controlling forces of livestock farming is agribusiness, how far are they answering to public demand? Undeniably, to some extent they are. There is public demand for animal produce, though how far the desire is innate and how far it is simply a cultural habit remains open to doubt. The question to ask, however, is whether the urge to consume animals is so great that it necessitates the slaughter of approximately 7 million chickens, 300,000 sheep, 300,000 pigs and 80,000 cows every week in this country?[8] Do humans have such an overpowering lust for animal protein that it overrides all considerations of suffering? Is the livestock industry slitting more throats and erecting bigger factory farms and slaughterhouses simply to answer this public lust? Personally, such a suggestion seems ridiculous. What the vested interests have done is to take a basic truth — most people associate some meat-eating with healthy, 'natural' and prosperous living — and use every tool the twentieth century has to offer in order to promote those associations.

Advertising has been their most powerful implement. In the year ending September 1981, figures revealed that the meat and poultry industries spent more than £36 million on promotion of their products.[9] (This figure also includes fish products.) Such vast sums of money would not be invested without good cause. Indeed, Buxted Chicken actually carried the revealing advertising slogan: 'Be sure. Stock the brand that creates the demand'. This suggests that the meat and poultry industries are only too well aware of their capacity to influence our diets.

Exactly how advertising helps to achieve this end remains something of a mystery, but there is little doubt that it does have enormous impact. Take, for instance, the recent example of Farmer's Table poultry. Farmer's Table is part of another multinational group, Fitch

Lovell, which also owns Keymarket and David Greig supermarkets. (Ties with retail outlets is another common feature of multinational food groups). Before Christmas 1981, they decided to advertise their turkeys on television for the first time. In response, Keymarket supermarkets reported a staggering 113 per cent increase in sales of Farmer's Table. Commenting, *Meat Magazine* was truthful enough to write that 'any medium which has an 18 million-strong audience must be right for commercial exploitation'.[10] Advertising (especially on television) combined with shop displays giving a particular product more prominence than others, can affect consumer demand enormously. Huge investments in both generic advertising (i.e. where a group of companies pay money to promote a type of food such as eggs or chicken), or alternatively, on a specific brand name (like Farmer's Table or Buxted) has been an important factor in the increase in animal protein consumption over the last 20 years. Every year, the sums invested in advertising escalate. In March 1982, Matteson's (part of Unilever) announced that they would spend £1 million in the following year.[11] Another subsidiary of the Unilever group, Walls Meat Co., revealed in the same week that they would be undertaking the biggest promotional spending by a single company in the history of meat production. The sum involved £2 million.[12]

In 1950, the average Briton consumed 0.35oz of chicken and 0.3oz of pork per person per week.[13] By 1981, the figures were 7.06oz and 4.13oz respectively.[14] Only 15 years ago chicken was a luxury, eaten at Christmas and perhaps one or two other holidays. Nowadays, the British public considers it a convenience food. By any standards, it is a remarkable change in such a short space of time. Can there be any real doubt that the demand has been stimulated largely by the vested interests themselves?

Of course, this explanation raises a further question. Even if it is true that big business is adept at dictating public taste, why exactly has so much emphasis been placed upon selling vast quantities of animal produce? Surely, the sceptic might argue, the reason so much money has been invested in animal produce is that fundamentally this is what the public wish to eat. We must recognize an element of truth in this argument. But we must also ask if there is a specific commercial explanation. There probably is. Indeed, it is the very reason that makes consumption of animal produce so uneconomic in terms of feeding the world population that constitutes its attraction to the multinationals.

Large food companies are predominantly concerned with profits and not with feeding people adequately or economically. Therefore, the great problem that they must overcome is that rapid expansion is quickly constrained by people's physical capacity to eat. If one is in the property business, one can sell more expensive homes as people get richer. If they become richer still, one can sell them second homes, and so on. This, in turn, creates opportunities for expansion in auxilliary trades — decorating, architecture, surveying, furnishings, etc. There is always room for more profits and greater expansion. The same principle can be applied to almost all trade — except food. Although people will consume larger quantities and more expensive food as income increases, they cannot eat *that* much more.

Consequently, in order to try and keep profits expanding, vested interests in food have to fight for extra shares of the market (e.g. the domination of the poultry industry by a few companies) or find food that maximizes profits. In *The Famine Business*, Colin Tudge explains how animal produce fits perfectly into this role.

> If he (the farmer) grows wealthy, invests more in production, produces more, he finds himself trying to sell five sacks of corn to people who are physiologically capable of consuming only one...
>
> Livestock provide the buffer, the sump to mop up surplus. Instead of trying to sell five sacks of corn to people who only want one, the farmer feeds four and a half to pigs and sells less corn than before, but with meat as well.
>
> And if people have a surfeit even of meat, he can begin to throw some of the carcase away: the offal and heads once prized, find their way into pet food. Thus, through the agency of meat, agriculture can expand indefinitely... it is meat production demanding roughly a tenfold loss in the human food available from a given area of land, that most spectacularly solves the paradox that production must increase if agricultural wealth is to keep pace with the rest of society, yet is theoretically constrained by people's ability to consume.[15]

To illustrate how vital animals have become to this process of max-imizing profits for the food industry, let us look at one specific ex-ample. By examining some of the activities of the Dalgety group, we can see further how multinational involvement in animal production is also directly related to their interests in other convenience foods. In this case, the bread industry.

In 1979, Dalgety took over Spillers, reportedly paying £73 million.[16] Spillers are one of three companies responsible for 80 per cent of the nation's flour supply, providing the raw materials for many of our bakeries. Most of the flour supplied is white and refined, suitable for the white sliced loaf. The flour producers and bread in-dustry claim that they produce this product in response to public de-mand, but there is a good deal of evidence to suggest that this is something of a myth. The demand is created by the same tactics employed by the meat and poultry industry. More white bread is sold mainly because the industry prefers it that way: there is more profit in it. Both bran and wheatgerm are removed from the grain during refining, making the final product less valuable nutritionally. As far as vested interests are concerned this has two advantages. Firstly, people need to eat more before they are satisfied; and secondly, the wheatgerm and bran can be sold elsewhere. In particular, bran and wheatgerm constitute an important source of protein in animal feed.

*Table 7.2* Dalgety/Spiller's ownership of poultry at time of takeover

| Name of Subsidiary | Number of birds |
| --- | --- |
| *Egg-laying hens* | |
| Deans Farm Eggs | 1 million |
| Macster Poultry | 200,000 |
| Sainsbury/Spiller (joint ownership) | 800,000 |
| *Broiler chickens* | |
| Kew House Farms | 6 million |
| Sainsbury/Spiller (joint ownership) | 170,000 |
| *Old-hen processors* | |
| E.B. Packers | 70,000 |
| *Turkeys* | |
| Swifts Poultry (joint ownership) | 400,000 |

*Source*: *Poultry Industry*, 1 November 1979

Since the Dalgety/Spillers organization also own approximately 13 per cent of the nation's supply of animal feedstuffs,[17] they hold a position from which they are well equipped to reap full benefit from the nation's 'preference' for white bread.

From here, the chain of vested interests is rather more predictable. Much of the animal feed provides Dalgety's own considerable involvement in factory farming of pigs and chickens — the latter alone said to be worth £60 million.[18] When the animals have been fattened, they may be transported by group company transport to one of the group's own slaughterhouses for processing. What happens to the slaughterhouse by-products like offal and heads? Conveniently, Spillers happen to be the largest suppliers of pet food in the country!

Thus, multinationals like Dalgety, by being involved at all levels of production, can ensure that every possible penny is extracted from the original grain. Yet although this process may seem a model of economic efficiency and is, undoubtedly, beneficial to company profit, its effect upon individual life is less advantageous. The cost to our factory-farmed animals has been documented in earlier chapters. In addition, it is accepted by even the most conservative nutritionists that the average British diet is now at least 20 per cent deficient in roughage and also contains 15 per cent more meat than is good for us.[19] Wheatgerm and bran put into bread rather than animal feed would go some way towards remedying this imbalance, but unfortunately it might also mean less profits for producers.

Meanwhile, evidence mounts that overconsumption of animal produce contributes strongly towards diseases of western civilization, particularly obesity, heart attacks and cancer of the bowel. In February 1983, The Health Education Council went so far as to sponsor full-page advertisements in national newspapers to offer a healthier diet for the population of the UK.[20] Putting responsibility for greater incidence of obesity on lack of fibre, the advertisement added that we should eat 'maybe half as much again' at the expense of meat, poultry, eggs, fish, dairy products and sugary things. To do so would reduce the risks of constipation, hernia, piles and diverticular disease. Further evidence was supplied by researchers at Liverpool University into victims of heart diseases at Royal Liverpool Hospital. As reported in the *Daily Mail* (30 March 1983), it was found that most sufferers ate more than four eggs a week and that meat consumption averaged

11 meat meals a week. The doctors concluded that there was a clear correlation between egg and meat consumption and heart disease, recommending people to eat a maximum of three eggs and four meat meals per week.

Given these facts it is no wonder that in the 1980 Reith Lectures, Professor Kennedy was moved to remark that 'the food industry has been enormously successful in ruining our diet and consequently our health'.[21]

Primarily, farm animals are not being bred and reared in their millions to fulfil either human need or insatiable human appetites for their flesh; they are being sacrificed in the cause of extra money for big business. They have become, in the words of Jim Mason and Peter Singer, 'the perfect cash crop',[22] turning inexpensive grain into high-price meat. It is a process that is helping to ruin the health of consumers as well as causing unquantifiable misery to millions of living creatures.

# 8. Myth three: the solution to world hunger

One of the popular lines of defence used by the factory farming industry to brush up its tarnished image is to present itself in a philanthropic light. Not content with its claim to produce cheap, wholesome and nutritious food for our own population, its publicity officers argue further that modern animal production is also helping to alleviate human hunger in poorer countries. When criticized on animal welfare grounds, responses like the following from the secretary of the International Egg Commission are not uncommon:

> We must counter their [the animal welfare movement] emotional arguments with emotional replies. Tell them about the hungry nations that are benefiting from the advances made by the poultry industry. They don't know it all — these budding St Francises.[1]

That was in 1979. In May 1981, the National Farmers' Union, resorting to the same argument (without the rallying rhetoric), issued a press notice entitled 'Farmers are the most important people in the world.' In it, President Sir Richard Butler, referred to the '100 million undernourished children under 5 years old' and asked for extra support for agriculture in order to 'set about the task of turning hunger into effective economic demand and expanding production to meet it'.

The task of this chapter is simply to squash, once and for all, the widely held belief that 'hungry nations' can benefit from 'advances' made by factory farming. On the contrary, our eating habits in the west actually contribute towards famine in underdeveloped nations and, more particularly, the introduction of similar food policies into poorer countries are totally inappropriate to the needs of those nations.

Without dwelling on what has been documented before, it must be established that, generally speaking, eating animal produce is an inefficient use of food resources. It involves feeding more protein-value to the animal in the form of grains than is eventually obtained from the carcase. This is because not all of the protein consumed by the animal can be digested and converted into meat. Much of the food value is lost in the process of digestion itself, and in cell replacement and other normal biological functions of animals. Table 8.1 gives some idea of how inefficient the protein conversion of livestock farming actually is.

*Table 8.1* Efficiency of livestock conversion of protein in whole-farm situations

|  | Protein conversion % |
|---|---|
| Dairy herd | 23 |
| Beef herd | 6 |
| Laying flock | 18 |

*Source*: P.G.C. Dum 'Intensive Farming – The Grand Delusion', adapted from L.K. Baxter, quoting Holmes, *Biologist,* vol. 23, 1976, p.14.

In answer to this, factory farming interests make much of the fact that through advances in genetic breeding they are able to produce animals that are increasingly more efficient converters of grain to meat. Yet even according to their own figures, the most efficient form of animal farming, (broiler chicken) still involves feeding 2.2kg of grain to obtain 1kg of meat. In real terms, meat production is considerably less efficient than such a figure suggests, because it takes no account of the inedible parts of the dead animal. For example, in broiler chicken production, blood, feet, head, guts and feathers are all removed, leaving only 44 per cent of the bird that is edible. Even allowing that the dressed chicken carcase provides more concentrated protein than the original vegetable food, the true conversion rate works out at about 9 – 10kg of feed to produce 1kg of meat, rather than the 2.2 to 1 that the industry claims.[2] In addition, any detailed assessment of the inefficiency of eating animal meat would also have to take into account other factors, such as losses during farming owing to high mortality rates. Whatever the exact figures, it is perfectly apparent 'that animals are not very efficient at producing protein for us from the protein we feed them'.[3] At a rough estimate, cereals grown to feed direct to humans will produce five times more protein per acre than if the same area was devoted to meat production; legumes average 10 times more and leafy vegetables 15 times more.[4]

These stark facts are often countered by the assertion that animal produce compensates for its ineffective food conversion rates by producing higher quality protein. At best, this is less than a half truth. When animals convert vegetable matter into meat, the protein is only slightly superior to that found in some cereals or cashew nuts or soya beans. Furthermore two sources of 'inferior' vegetable proteins, such as pulses and grains, can complement each other in providing a protein intake every bit as valuable as meat. Meat-eating is both wasteful and unnecessary. As Professor Kenneth Mellanby stated during the 1979 Poultry Industry Conference, most nutritionalists now accept that animal protein has no unique value. At the same time production of animal protein diminishes the possibility of feeding the world's population adequately.

To be fair, however, these arguments do not mean that from a purely food-producing viewpoint, universal vegetarianism is necessarily the answer to the problem of human hunger. Although this concept may be morally attractive, it has to be admitted that there are two circumstances where animal production does not result in food wastage. Firstly, when ruminant animals — sheep, cattle, goats — are able to convert leaf protein which is unsuitable for human consumption into edible food. On marginal lands and uplands, where cultivation of crops is impossible, the rearing of these animals can be justified on the grounds of efficiency. They are producing food where otherwise there would be nothing. Secondly, omnivores such as pigs and chickens, which are often fed on food suitable for human consumption, can be kept in small numbers on kitchen leftovers. The backyard pig or chicken offers another example where animal production is not wasteful.

What little livestock keeping there is in the poorer areas of developing nations normally falls into one of these two categories — a few backyard poultry, a pig raised on scrap, or perhaps a few sheep or goats kept on a wild hillside. Preaching vegetarianism in opposition to such customs is totally inappropriate. One cannot expect people whose lives are dominated by the effort of scraping together enough food for survival to be impressed by moral or philosophical arguments in favour of vegetarianism. In addition, these practices are essentially irrelevant to our present purpose, since in terms of world food production the amounts of animal produce involved are minimal. Unlike factory farmers, subsistence farmers would never divert food fit for humans into the stomachs of animals; the difference is that the latter are concerned with feeding themselves, the former with making profits.

In summary, we can say that animals have only limited food-producing value in their ability to convert coarse fodder unsuitable for humans. As a general policy, it is vital that we rely increasingly upon vegetable protein in our diets if we are to feed a world population which is expanding rapidly. In fact, if the world's grain harvest was fed directly to humans, there would be more than enough to feed current levels of population.

Let us compare the necessity of feeding everyone, with what is actually happening in the world. To clarify the position, we can divide the human world into two types of areas, developed and underdeveloped. Firstly, in the developed world, by which we mean principally North America, Oceania and western and eastern Europe (including the USSR), we see, without exception a significant increase in animal production, particularly in western Europe. In the years 1961-65, 62 per cent of the cereal grown in this region was fed to animals, whilst only 38 per cent went directly to humans. The last available figures show that between 1975-77 the figure had risen to 70 per cent of cereal for animal feed, leaving only 30 per cent for direct human consumption.[5] Ever-increasing areas of land have been devoted to growing animal feed at the expense of food for humans. For reasons we shall discuss later, the developed world is eating progressively more meat. In Britain, Gerald Leach calculated that by 1972, only 8 per cent of our cultivated land was used to grow food directly.[6] Most of the remainder was turned over to feed for livestock. Farming interests make much of the fact that, according to Ministry of Agriculture figures, Britain has now reached 70 per cent self-sufficiency in food production. Yet such achievements appear very insignificant when one realizes that theoretically, we are capable of sustaining a population of 250 million people on an all-vegetable diet. Our present population is approximately 56 million.

Therefore, self-sufficiency could be achieved easily without resorting to total vegetarianism.

It will be questioned whether in practice it makes any difference to developing nations whether or not the western world continues to consume ever-increasing amounts of animal produce. The answer is that it does, in two essential ways. In Britain, as we have already seen, the existence of factory farming demands that stock are fattened up as quickly as possible at the cheapest possible cost. To achieve this end, they must be fed on special high-protein diets. Consequently, animal feed companies scour the world in search of the cheapest source of protein that fits the bill. Every year, the amount of animal feeding stuff imported into the UK shows an increase. In 1980 the figure was 1,335 million tonnes.[7] The majority of this consists of grains from America and Europe, and soya also from America. Much is made of western aid to the third world, yet the fact is that nearly all the developed world's vast agricultural wealth is geared towards fattening imprisoned animals, not feeding hungry children. There is more money in animals. For instance, only one-tenth of the vast acreage of soya beans harvested in the USA is fed to humans; more than half finds its way to western Europe for animal feed.[8]

Admittedly, the concept of direct food aid to third world nations may well be limited, especially in so far as it makes no essential contribution towards solving the long-term economic problems of the receiver. Nevertheless, as a short-term measure in times of severe famine it remains the only possibility of relief. Unfortunately, whilst present-day policies of ever-increasing meat production continue, then all the money in the world devoted to agriculture will do nothing to alleviate human hunger in the poorer countries. On the contrary, it will simply mean more land turned over to animal feed, more factory farms and more meat-eating in the west.

The developed world perpetuates worse crimes against the third world than simply selfishly wasting its own resources. George Borstrom has estimated that developed nations are 'acquiring from the hungry world 1 million metric tonnes more protein than is delivered to the hungry world through grain'.[9] We take more than we give. Approximately 3½ million tonnes of high-protein foodstuff is imported by industrialized countries from developing countries every year; roughly speaking, enough to meet the nutritional needs of 300 million humans.[10] The majority is used either for feeding livestock or for pet food. Britain is by no means the worst exploiter of this cheap source of protein, yet in recent years we have imported sunflower, groundnut meal and cakes, and other oil-seed protein — potential famine-relief food — from poor countries like Sudan, Senegal, Ethiopia, India, Tanzania and Gambia.[11] Although this trade has been greatly reduced in the last few years following the discovery of potentially dangerous levels of aflatoxins in groundnut meal — which effectively curtailed trade in what was previously the chief source of imported protein for animal feed from the third world — it remains to be seen whether problems will be overcome sufficiently to encourage resumption of trade in the future.[12] Groundnut meal is the high-protein residue processed after oil has been extracted from the nuts. It can and has been used successfully in Indian famine-relief programmes as the chief ingredient in a nutritional liquid food, added to locally grown starch, vitamins and minerals.[13]

Sometimes it is not directly a case of food that should feed humans going to animals, but rather that land in third world countries is used to grow 'cash crops' when it could be more profitably utilized in the production of grains or pulses with higher nutritional value. For instance, the most popular source of cheap animal feed from the third world at present is manioc (tapioca), basically a starch product imported mostly from Thailand. Over the last decade, Thailand has increased production from 3 million to 13 million tonnes per annum.[14] It is purchased by livestock farmers throughout Europe because it remains far cheaper than home-grown cereals. At the same time as our arable farmers are paid subsidies by the EEC (out of taypayers' money) to take their unwanted cereals off the market and into intervention stores, more land in Thailand is devoted to growing manioc at the expense of crops which might alleviate falling standards of nutrition in the native population.

At the beginning of 1983, measures were at last introduced in the EEC to alter this ludicrous situation by controlling the quotas of manioc allowed in animal feed. Sensible though this decision is, it can only be seen as a short-term measure, offering no solutions to the real problem of the dependence of the west upon poorer countries in order to satisfy our taste for luxury. Indeed, an added problem for the third world is likely to be created by animal feed companies switching their interest from one crop to another, depending solely upon economic motives. Having geared its agricultural production towards western desires, any poorer nation which happens to be discarded in favour of a better deal elsewhere may find its markets disappearing overnight, resulting in considerable chaos amongst the agricultural community. Basically, the only answer is for the third world to concern itself with feeding its own population directly; and for the west to allow it to do so.

It might be argued that, for political reasons, food would not find its way into hungry mouths even if developed countries did prohibit the import of high protein feed. But this is simply an evasion of responsibility. Our obligation is to offer poorer nations real opportunities to develop their own resources; whereas, at present, what limited effort is made to assist is often at best hopelessly misdirected and at worse little more than a public relations exercise, as in the following quotation:

> Pacific-coast Latin Americans are frequently hungry and may suffer protein deficiency. Their fishermen catch anchovies, but Latin American do not eat this high-protein diet, because they cannot afford the price. Instead they put them in ships and send them to Denmark. The Danes don't eat them, but feed them to pigs — and then send cans of pork as food aid to Latin America.[15]

Although not the main reason, it is no coincidence that at the same time as the meat and poultry industries in industrialized nations have expanded dramatically, there has been an increase in the number of undernourished people on earth. The Food and Agricultural Organization estimates that in 1969-71 there were 360 million people without enough food to meet their minimum nutritional requirements. By 1980, that figure had risen to 490 million.[16] This disturbing fact is often dismissed on the grounds that world population is increasing so fast that food production cannot possibly keep up with it. In other words, whatever the west chooses to consume is ultimately irrelevant since there is an insurmountable problem of too many mouths to feed. This is simply another red herring.

In fact, during the last 20 years, world food supply has considerably outgrown population growth. In 1963, the available food on earth was only 1 per cent greater than the theoretical nutritional requirements of mankind. By 1972-74, this had been transformed into an estimated 7 per cent worldwide food surplus, increasing annually. Indeed, by 1977, food supplies in developing nations as a whole were themselves estimated equal to the minimum requirements for adequate health of their own peoples.[17] It goes without saying that theory and reality are miles apart, taking no account of maldistribution both between and within countries, nor of many other political and economic factors. Nevertheless, these figures are useful as an indication that our potential to fight famine is increasing, not diminishing. The contrasting fact that more people starve every year is proof enough that western eating habits are unacceptable.

The developing world also shows an increase overall in the amounts of cereals grown for feeding animals, but only in Latin America (where 41 per cent of cereals produced during 1975/77 went to animal feed compared to 32 per cent a decade earlier) is the increase dramatic. Part of this exception can be attributed to policies in the USA, which uses land in Central America to fatten up beef for import. The expansion of beef production in Latin America has not necessarily coincided with larger quantities of meat being available to the native population.[18] In other poor continents there has been little change: 2 per cent more cereal fed to animals in Africa; 1 per cent more in the Near East; a 2 per cent more reduction in Asia, and no change in the Far East.

These figures emphasize that meat remains the food of the rich. Where there is great hardship, little or no animal produce is consumed. As income increases, however, people usually consume increasing amounts of meat. Even if we partly accept the argument that this progression is explained by an innate desire for animal flesh, it is a simplification to claim this as the sole reason. There are other factors involved, both political and psychological. Just as meat-eating came to symbolize improved financial security for individual families in post-war Britain, following times of austerity, so it is easily understood why developing nations should look upon animal produce as an important sign of economic growth. If one had been accustomed to harsh poverty and struggle, it is natural to be impressed by and aspire to the standards of those who seem to have more than enough and infinite choice. Meat-eating on a large scale is a symbol of affluence in the industrialized nations, enthusiastically pursued by the poorer half of the world.

Naturally, this desire for emulation is good news for the governments of richer countries who are always on the lookout for new export markets. Since most developed nations rely more or less upon the same agricultural policies — continuous corn-growing to fatten up animals in factory farms — it is extremely difficult for them to create new markets for the ingredients which sustain these systems — advanced technology, animal genetics, and chemicals — within their own half of the world. Therefore, poorer countries remain the most potent source of new trade for both agribusiness and western governments. Their collusion can be illustrated conclusively by glancing at the lists of 'experts' who accompany overseas trade missions undertaken by the Ministry of Agriculture.

For example, on 23 September 1981, the Minister of Agriculture, Peter Walker, returned from a 10-day tour of Argentina and Brazil and issued a press notice in the usual aggressive terms. The gist of his statement was that Argentina has 'enormous scope for high levels of production', Brazil is providing 'a fast-expanding consumer market' and 'our share of the market could double or treble with effort and application'.[19] Amongst those accompanying him on the tour were representatives of Booker Agriculture, a firm whose self-avowed principle activity is 'agribusiness with emphasis on poultry genetics'. They also own Arbor Acres Farm, one of the world's market leaders in producing chicks for the broiler industry, and Nicholas Turkeys, the biggest producers of turkey breeding stock in the world. Then, two weeks before the Minister's trip to South America, Earl Ferrers, Minister of State at the Ministry of Agriculture, was off to Saudi Arabia, the Yemen Arab Republic and Egypt on another export promotion. Two of the six businessmen with him were connected with livestock farming, one of them a part of Imperial Foods Ltd, at that time Britain's largest poultry producers.[20]

Of course, there is nothing wrong with such an arrangement in principle. Moral problems arise only when the goods that big business have to sell overseas are inappropriate to the need of the receiving nations. Unfortunately, this is precisely the category that factory farming falls into.

Factory farming, particularly of poultry, is sweeping across the whole of the developing world, from Africa to Asia. Perhaps the most ludicrous example can be found in Bangladesh, which remains amongst the poorest countries in the world, densely overpopulated and with infant mortality as high as 125 children in every 1,000 live births.[21] Astonishingly, in 1979, Bangladesh added its name to the long list of developing nations embarking upon battery farming. A firm called Phoenix Poultry Ltd received a Bangladesh government grant equivalent to approximately £⅓ million to set up a unit for 6,000 broiler birds and 18,000 laying hens.[22] By western standards this is a small investment, but for Bangladesh it represents enormous expansion. Previous estimates put the total number of hens in the country at only 35,000,[23] none of which would have been kept intensively.

Announcing this expansion, *Poultry World* magazine heralded it as a sign of Bangladesh's economic recovery. In fact, it is a sign of total insanity. Bangladesh has no capital to spare, extremely poor energy resources, huge surpluses of manpower, and massive shortages of food.[24] Intensive chicken rearing demands a huge outlay of capital for buildings, machinery, etc.; extensive use of energy resources for automation; requires little human labour (one of its attractions to the industrialized nations being that it reduces manpower costs); and involves feeding birds with potential famine-relief protein food which they then inefficiently convert into meat or eggs.

An article in the journal of the Food and Agricultural Organization, *Ceres*, explains how the lunch bowl of agricultural labourers in Bangladesh contains 'a modest helping of plain boiled rice without meat, vegetables or even sauce'. Look in his wife's bowl or in the bowl of the man who cannot find work and you will find half that quantity.[25] Yet here we have the Bangladesh government financing a scheme guaranteed to reduce the amount of food grains available to people and supporting a system which will not create any extra work for the enormous number of unemployed. At present, Bangladesh has to import four times more than it exports. One of the chief imports is food grains, because the country is unable to grow enough food to feed its own population. On what then, do they intend to feed the chickens? Presumably they will have to pay to import grains to feed them? And when the birds have inefficiently converted the grains into meat or eggs, who will be able to eat them?

Obviously not the agricultural worker who cannot even afford a few vegetables with his bowl of rice. As for his wife or the unemployed, they will have even less opportunity of sampling the finished results of factory farming. In fact, the only people able to benefit — if that is the right word — will be the wealthy minority; the poverty stricken will be left with even less food available than before.

Without technology and equipment from developed nations it would be impossible for the third world to imitate our factory farm systems. In the case of Bangladesh, equipment was supplied and installed by Japanese, Danish and British companies. In addition to ensuring that Bangladesh is now committed to methods of farming totally inapplicable to its needs, this also means that the recipient country is dependent on western technologies, since it is unlikely that such a 'backward' nation will possess either the parts or the knowledge necessary to cope with any problems which may occur. Like many other overseas development programmes, this is likely to prove advantageous to the donor country, but no help to the receiver.

India has a much more established poultry industry. In 1960 she had a small egg industry from hens kept in backyards, but no broiler chickens. By 1979, her annual egg production had reached 12 million eggs, and 24 million broilers were reared. According to *Poultry Industry*, 'widespread increase in intensive poultry keeping'[26] has been largely responsible. Predictions for the future suggest continuous expansion on a massive scale. By the Indian poultry industry's own admission, factory farming has had little effect on malnutrition. The difficulties are much the same as in Bangladesh, particularly the inability of poor people to purchase luxury foods.[27] Therefore, only the wealthy buy poultry that has been reared on valuable vegetable and fish proteins. In fact, consumer demand for poultry is so low in India that despite her overwhelming problems of malnutrition, she has begun to export eggs and chickens, mostly to the Gulf states!

Yet again, Britain, along with other industrialized nations, has played its part in these developments. The multinational firm Unilever, through their associates in India, have a network of feed manufacturing units which are the largest in the country. Ross Breeders Ltd, part of the same Imperial group which dominated the British poultry market, also have a major project there. It is remarkable how often the names of multinationals with British connections are involved in third world intensive farming schemes, usually the same firms which are responsible for our own factory farming. In particular, Ross Breeders supply birds all over the world. They have recently extended their business into the Far East, following a deal to link up with four other companies in producing a 'broiler breeding complex' from which they hope eventually to breed 100 million broiler chicks per annum for Malaysia.[28]

The Malaysian poultry industry offers another rags-to-riches story. It has developed from a 'background enterprise' to a multimillion dollar business in the last 25 years. A recent poultry magazine article on this 'progression' was enthusiastically entitled 'Malaysia reaches self-sufficiency in poultry meat'.[29] The article went on to explain that the area no longer has to import chicken meat for its population; instead she imports 80,000 tonnes of feed grains to feed her chickens! Certainly it is a strange concept of self-sufficiency when Malaysia still has to feed chickens on imported soya bean meal, maize, barley, and wheat.

The area of greatest expansion for factory farms has, not surprisingly, been the Middle East. Almost all Gulf states have built up their poultry industry to massive proportions in the last decade, helped inevitably by western technology. Hardly a month goes by without news of a new poultry complex utilizing British birds or equipment. One of the biggest deals in 1981 involved Iraq. GKN Engineering and Ross Poultry together won a contract worth £21 million to build a poultry unit north of Baghdad. The scale of investment seems to grow with each new deal.

As yet, it is only intensive poultry keeping that has been established on a large scale in poorer nations; but we have only to examine the history of factory farming in the UK to grasp how the concept is certain to spread to other farm animals. Although factory farming of pigs is not yet established on an international scale, by 1980 the UK was already exporting pigs 'for breeding purposes' to Taiwan, Malaysia, Thailand, the Malagasy Republic, Nigeria and Zambia.[30] Who can argue with any conviction that intensive piggeries will not proliferate throughout the third world during the next few years?

The spread of intensive farming does not offer the most dramatic example of the ways in which western governments exploit poorer nations, but it is inextricably connected with more blatant demonstrations of greed and profiteering. For instance, the way that our 'milk lakes' have lead to the overseas sales of 'extra high-protein babyfoods':

> Tragic are the attempts by third world mothers who waste half their incomes trying to nourish their infants on such food, whilst their breasts dry up and the produce of the sur-rounding fields − which could help the mothers in lactation − is channelled into European piggeries.[31]

Whilst it would be ridiculous to blame factory farming for caus-ing the enormous inequalities in the world, it is, nevertheless, part and parcel of the way that rich nations continue to use underdeveloped areas as 'an udder to feed its supreme selves'. Although conditions and specific problems vary enormously from country to country, it is a fact that the basic principle of factory farming is irreconcilable with helping the fight against human hunger in poverty-stricken areas. The developed nations must continue to help the poverty stricken with direct food aid during emergencies; but more importantly, we must encourage a technology which the native population are able to con-trol themselves in order to bring greater areas under cultivation and improve existing yields. It must be a technology that creates employ-ment and does not simply replace people with machines. Where animals do already play a role in third world economies we must teach respect and compassion, not imitation of our callousness. (We should not fall into the trap of glorifying the treatment of animals in poorer nations. Brutality is common.) Above all, western nations can assist by allowing the third world to base food production on its own needs rather than our taste for luxury, and individually, we can all play a part by living according to principles worthy of imitation − morally, economically and ecologically. Cutting out all factory farm produce and at least minimizing present-day meat-eating habits are crucial.

Rather than helping to alleviate human hunger and misery, fac-tory farming contributes towards it. Its application in the third world demonstrates conclusively that when people throw up the common arguement, 'why care about factory-farmed animals when there are so many starving people in the world?' they have not investigated the issues involved. Were they to do so, they would find the same heartless principles of greed and profit before life and compassion are responsible for both.

# 9. Myth four: happy workers

With a surplus of capital available, big business likes to invest its money-power in advanced technology rather than human labour because in the long term it provides cheaper goods. It also gives competitive advantages over smaller producers who lack the capital to lay out on expensive machines. The principal effect of this on animal farming has been that the number of stock workers employed has diminished rapidly over the past 30 years. In the words of former EEC Commissioner on Agriculture, Dr Siccio Mansholt, 'because of investment in modern technological equipment, capital wishes to exclude human labour'.[1]

It would be wrong to attribute these trends solely to the pervasive presence of big business. Advanced technology replacing human labour has become a feature of almost all areas of twentieth-century life, and the causes are complex. Neither would it be justifiable to assume that all these developments are necessarily detrimental to either animals or human workers. Technology can be used to make life better for both. Having acknowledged this, however, there is, when it comes to factory farming, a profound correlation between the destructive consequences for animals and the soul-destroying quality of human work that often accompanies it. As observed in *The Famine Business*, 'Modern intensive pig and poultry units have a high labour turnover precisely because the job, though perhaps requiring little muscle power, is physically and mentally so debilitating.'[2] This statement points to the way in which factory farming tends to exploit all life, not only the lives of farm animals.

It is ironic that although modern methods have resulted in many millions more birds and thousands of extra animals now being reared for food, the number of stock workers employed to look after them has greatly dwindled. Not so long ago, the idea of one man or woman looking after more than 1,500 hens would have been ridiculed. Nowadays, on battery farms, that same person would have control over at least 20,000 birds. Similarly, one man may now be in charge of the welfare of hundreds of pigs.

Inevitably, these developments have destroyed any possibility of either individual attention for the animals or any meaningful rapport between animals and stockworker. Although the Welfare of Livestock Regulations (1978) makes it compulsory for all farm animals to be inspected at least once a day, one does not have to be a time and motion expert to realize that even the most perfunctory glance at 20,000 hens or 1,000 pigs is likely to take a considerable length of time. Much longer, in fact, than most workers will have available. This was the reason why, in 1982, the RSPCA took a court case against a battery hen owner who, over a period of two nights and one day, spent only 9½ minutes checking his birds.[3] An official of the RSPCA added that the prosecution was not brought because of any deliberate cruelty by the particular farmer; on the contrary, the significance of the case was that it was so typical of all battery hen producers.

According to defenders of factory farming, the fact that the ratio of human workers to number of animals has been reduced so dramatically is considered a great economic advantage. But it has to be emphasized that it is an advantage *only* to producers. With unemployment figures soaring, it seems ludicrous to suggest that there are not enough workers available to look after animals in more humane conditions. Moreover, a move towards labour-intensive husbandry would unquestionably also allow greater care for individual animals. In the words of Professor Spedding, head of the Agricultural Department at Reading University:

> There is little doubt that employing more people to look after animals can help to reduce losses from disease and mortality of the newborn in particular.[4]

Sometimes the argument that 'efficiency' dictates the replacement of humans by machines is reinforced by the suggestion that workers actually prefer conditions in battery houses to those in less intensive systems, as in the following quotation from an article, 'Cages best for owners, workers, consumers and birds':

It has to be a subjective decision as to which type of system is preferable to work in, but there is no doubt that recruiting the much larger labour force needed for any of the alternatives, who themselves would require greater animal husbandry skills, would prove extremely difficult nowadays.

In other words, the battery system would seem to suit todays smaller number of people prepared to work with stock and to endure the physical exertion and discomfort associated with keeping stock under less sophisticated systems, perhaps exposed to the elements.[5]

The weakness of the argument is illustrated clearly by the exaggerated denigration of working with animals outside. Phrases like 'exposed to the elements' and 'physical exertion and discomfort' give an unbalanced and biased viewpoint, unsupported by the evidence.

In fact, if we look at debates and discussions on modern farming where stockworkers are asked for their preference, it emerges that the majority much prefer farming outdoors to keeping animals in cages and crates. For instance, Joan Maynard MP made this comment during a House of Commons debate on battery cages for laying hens:

Some people argue that stockmen prefer to look after battery hens indoors. That has not been the experience of my union. We have found that the majority of stockmen prefer to work out of doors. After all, that is why most of them decide to work in agriculture. It is certainly not for the wages they draw at the end of the week... The stockmen consulted by the union asked that considerable thought be given to stocking density. They stated that heat and dust seem always to be present in intensive poultry houses. The dust cannot be good either for the birds or for the men who work there, and it is no wonder that the incidence of respiratory diseases amongst farm workers is increasing... Most farm workers therefore find battery cages objectionable.[6]

Reading through the farming press it is apparent that this preference is not confined only to those working with hens. Not only do the health risks associated with factory farming turn staff against it; they also speak more positively of the enjoyment derived from working with animals outdoors. For example, Leslie Hill, a pig farmer from Somerset: 'But the chief reason for the outdoor system is that I prefer it, as does my pig man.'[7] Headley Hawkins, manager of the large Baxter-Parker Pig Enterprise in Norfolk, goes even further:

> Staff are happy with the system and many prefer working on range rather than in intensive houses. When people are happy so are the pigs, and our experience has been that you invariably have more problems with people than you have with pigs.[8]

It may be a simplification to associate happy pigs with happy people but at least Mr Hawkins alerts us to the possible benefits both people and animals can derive from working in an environment where there is a living relationship between them. He recognizes the communal element in any meaningful enterprise involving humans and other animals. Stockworkers and animals interact; their actions and attitudes influence each other. It should not be simply a case of humans fattening up a product for the dinner table.

A further illustration of the possible benefits of such relationships is provided by another free-range pig farmer from Devon:

> The feeding routine is a little slower outdoors. And at farrowing I balance the litters. But the time spent looking after the pigs outdoors is time pleasantly spent.
>
> I like the outdoor system, and because of that I do not mind spending the extra half an hour or so with it.[9]

Here we see a farmer who does not measure his occupation solely by profit margins. Contentment, work satisfaction, time pleasantly spent, awareness that there is enjoyment to be gained from associating with animals, are all unquantifiable factors which tend to be ignored by factory farmers, who have no opportunity to see animals as anything other than things to produce food. Inevitably, factory farming epitomizes what E.F. Schumacher refers to as 'the crude materialist viewpoint' of agriculture:

> The crude materialist view sees agriculture as 'essentially directed towards food production'. A wider view sees

agriculture as having to fulfil at least three tasks:

1. to keep man in touch with living nature, of which he is and remains a highly vulnerable part;
2. to humanize and ennoble man's wider habitat; and
3. to bring forth the foodstuffs and other material which are needed for a becoming life.

I do not believe that a civilization which recognizes only the third of these tasks, and which pursues it with such ruthlessness and violence, that the other two tasks are not merely neglected but systematically counteracted, has any chance of long-term survival.[10]

The nature of human labour that accompanies factory farming methods does worse damage than failing 'to keep man in touch with living nature'; in many cases it also demands that human responsiveness and sympathy are kept to a minimum. The person in charge is simply a press-button mechanic and on the more automated units, the more mechanically he performs his task, then the better it suits the system: 'A well-trained monkey could grow broilers. Indeed, it is often better with that sort of person, as long as there is good management to tell him what to do.'[11] This statement from a broiler farmer with 20 years' experience draws full attention to what he considers, quite literally, to be the subhuman nature of rearing broiler chicken. 'A well-trained monkey' is often better than a responsive human being.

Ultimately, the philosophies of factory farming and being a good stockworker are irreconcilable. Although conditions vary enormously between the best and the worst of factory farms, and many farmers do their utmost within the limitations of the system to ensure that animals are clean, warm and well fed, it is basically only the difference between a benevolent prison guard and an indifferent one. In the past, the careful working with animals was considered the secret of good husbandry; nowadays it is a dying art, uneconomic according to modern agricultural thinking.

Despite the fact that all farms have reduced their labour force, both the meat and poultry industries continue to refer to themselves as creators of jobs. This is because the tremendous increase in the number of animals reared for food has produced new jobs in the processing and packing industry. Whilst fewer people are employed to look after living creatures, many more take part in slaughtering and cutting up carcases.

Chapter 3 looked at the work of slaughterers in red-meat abattoirs; here, we examine the quality of work in poultry processing plants, where tasks vary between the nasty and the obscene. The nature of most of the tasks is summarized in the words of one poultry producer, responsible for the slaughter of 130,000 birds every week. Commenting on the high turnover of poultry meat inspectors, he said: 'It is not much fun watching chicken giblets going past you all day. For the first half hour or so it's not too bad, but then the machine takes over, as the line goes past you get mesmerized.'[12] Mechanization is only one of the problems. For others the work is both physically wearing and gory, as well as mentally debilitating. Jobs include taking birds out of crates and hanging them upside down on the shackles line; slitting throats or acting as back-up slaughterer to the automatic knives; and removing pieces of gut from each carcase as the dead birds pass by speedily on the fast-moving conveyor belt.

It is no surprise to find that an industry which treats birds without a shred of compassion is also recognizably indifferent to human welfare. Mr Jack Body, secretary of the National Union of Amalgamated Agricultural Workers, has in recent years, launched several severe attacks upon the poultry trade, alleging that its record on health, safety and welfare of workers 'stinks'.[13] In one speech Mr Body accused the industry of producing 'boring jobs, spartan, smelly, dirty and dangerous conditions and authoritarian management'.[14] He pointed to the high incidence of injuries caused by dangerous machinery moving too fast; illnesses such as tenosynovitis (which can cause permanent deformities of the hands and wrist as a result of being subjected to repetitive work at too fast a rate); wart-infested hands; and respiratory and eye diseases.[15] Long hours, unpleasant working conditions, the relentless speed of the processing line and the repetitive nature of the work, also cause a whole range of minor complaints ranging from backache to chilblains. Yet despite the obscenities, the current fears of unemployment ensure that the poultry industry continues to win support against protesters with the argument that a reduction in slaughter would result in loss of opportunities for human employment. Such a viewpoint has no foundation in fact because any reduction or even abandonment of mass processing of animals must inevitably be replaced by production of other food. People would still have to eat; therefore, alternative employment would be created in processing more varieties of vegetable proteins. This is discussed further in Part 3 of this book. The change from traditional farming to the factory production of animals represents one of the worst examples available of the possibility of meaningful work being destroyed in order to make profits for a minority. Whilst working with living animals is not an occupation that would suit everybody, it could provide relatively rewarding jobs for a significant minority of the unemployed, if the opportunity existed. But nowadays there is more possibility of employment by turning live animals into products on the supermarket shelf. By no stretch of the imagination can such a change be interpreted as progress. On the contrary, it is evident that if anybody is benefiting from factory farming, it is certainly not the human beings employed to operate the systems.

# 10. Myth five: economic necessity

When all else fails, defenders of factory farming always fall back upon their supreme defence — economics. Battery production is, we are assured, the only possible way of feeding our present population without sending food prices soaring astronomically. This viewpoint is so popular nowadays that its use is no longer confined to 'experts'. One is as likely to hear it put forward by the ubiquitous man or woman in the street as by highly qualified agricultural economists. From all quarters we are told authoritatively, sometimes even apologetically, that there is no economic alternative to factory farming. And since 'in the current vocabulary of condemnation there are few words as final and conclusive as the word uneconomic',[1] any alternatives, however preferable they might be to the quality of our lives, are dismissed.

Given that many economists have adopted methods of analysis outside the comprehension of non-experts (largely ignoring the effects of their statistics, upon individual life), it is worthwhile, here, making a few observations which must raise doubts about whether current practices are as efficient at producing cheap food as the status quo would have us believe. Before doing so, however, there is an important moral question to consider. If factory farming is proven cruel to animals, can it, under any circumstances be justified on economic grounds? According to our civilization, it most certainly can be, as exemplified by the much-quoted Protection of Birds Act (1954). This states that:

> If any person keeps or confines any bird whatsoever in any cage or other receptacle which is not sufficient in height, length or breadth to permit the bird to stretch its wings free- ly, he shall be guilty of an offence against the Act, and be

liable to a special penalty... Provided that this subsection shall not apply to poultry.[2]

This gives rise to the question: in the case of factory farming, how far is economics merely a word used to rationalize what mankind instinctively understands to be morally unacceptable — a sort of modern day religious justification of evil? The present codes of practice on farm animals in this country, suggest that it is an offence to cause 'unnecessary pain or distress'.[3] Yet some legal experts consider that in order to bring about a sucessful prosecution, it would be insufficient merely to prove that it was 'unnecessary'. The farmer could claim that his need for money makes a certain amount of cruelty permissible. If this is so, then it is clear that making money may override moral considerations. Under certain circumstances, cruelty may be legalized.

But what of the consumers? A popular argument is that even if factory farming is primarily a good way of making profits for producers, it is also practised for the economic benefit of the public, since without these methods, surely only the rich would be able to purchase large quantities of animal produce? It is this type of thinking that leads vested interests to call animal welfare societies 'the enemy of the housewife'.[4] Tending to ignore any moral or philosophical considerations, they argue instead that factory farming is the only possible way of feeding us all adequately. But is it? Confining the argument strictly to economic factors, we must now turn our attention to this issue: is factory farming as cheap as it seems?

From the outset it has to be admitted that under present circumstances, battery production may well be the cheapest way of supplying massive quantities of animal protein, but only because it is the most profitable method of taking advantage of current policies of agricultural support. A few of the financial incentives available to modern agriculture are described below, with their effects on current factory farming practices.

## Rate exemption

All farmers are exempt from paying rates on farm buildings. This concession was granted back in 1929 to help farmers survive a time of great economic depression. It was not, however, intended to allow new 'factory' buildings to proliferate all over our countryside. Although factory farming is not solely responsible for the estimated £150 million[5] that this concession costs the country, it is certainly the type of agricultural enterprise most undeserving of rate exemption. In the words of a recent Royal Commission on Environmental Pollution, intensive farms are 'essentially industrial enterprises and should be treated as such'.[6] Why then should a 20,000-bird battery unit, or a 300-sow pig unit escape the considerable rating burden met by commercial companies classified as 'light industrial'?

## Pollution control

Large flocks or herds of closely confined animals produce an enormous amount of excreta. On factory farms the area of farm land around the units is often insufficient to take the load. For instance, at least one-quarter of the pig units are on holdings where there is not enough arable land to make use of the manure.[7] Often, particularly when the waste is in liquid slurry form (as on most intensive pig farms) the smell is 'highly offensive' and 'penetrating'.[8]

These were two of the reasons which led the Royal Commission to conclude that 'pollution risks' in factory farms are 'subsequently greater than those arising from traditional agriculture'.[9] In all, the pollution load produced by the present level of farm animals is equivalent to 150 million humans.[10] But whereas human sewerage must be treated before being returned to the land, animal waste from intensive units is allowed back without any treatment. Although methods do exist for the treatment of slurry and to reduce smell, the Royal Commission concluded that 'in spite of the considerable efforts that have been expended, these techniques appear to have been adopted to only a negligent extent on farms in this country'.[11]

Industry has to meet the cost of pollution control, so why should factory farms escape it?

## Capital allowances

Farmers are allowed tax relief for capital expenditure on both agricultural buildings and machinery.[12]

For new buildings, they are allowed 30 per cent relief on construction costs and allowances of 10 per cent in each of the succeeding seven years, adding up to total exemption.[13]

It is true that similar concessions are offered to all commercial enterprises. The difference is that on the one hand, farming claims that its unique character should entitle it to special treatment (i.e. rate exemption) and on the other, it still wants to be treated like everybody else when it comes to possible financial advantages.

## Avoidance of capital gains tax

Farmers with either breeding stock, or animals kept primarily for the sale of their produce (e.g. milk or eggs) rather than for their flesh, are able to escape paying capital gains tax on profits made through buying and selling animals.[14] In theory, none of these concessions show any favour to factory farms. In practice they greatly encourage them. Tax relief on machinery and buildings, plus exemption from rates, means that after the initial capital cost is laid out, there are enormous advantages available that less sophisticated outdoor farmers cannot benefit from. The two main needs for an outdoor enterprise are land and labour — both increasingly expensive and largely unsupported by grants. On the other hand, intensive units basically exclude land and manpower and replace them with buildings and machinery — both of which *are* supported indirectly by grants. Factory farmers can set up a 100-sow pig-breeding unit on an acre of concrete and qualify for a 100 per cent capital allowance over a period of years. Roughly 15 acres would be needed for the same size herd outdoors, and the total tax relief available would be far lower, because buildings and machinery would both be extremely basic.

We can see that tax concessions encourage the farmer to use sophisticated technology. The only draw-back for the potential battery entrepreneur is the enormous capital needed to begin with, and this is precisely why big business and finance companies have come to dominate our agriculture. They have the capital available to buy units outright, to negotiate massive bank loans or to lend to farmers.

Another predominant feature of factory farms is their size. Units grow bigger and bigger, the growth tending to coincide with an increase in intensification. Obviously, one of the reasons for this is simply that you can cram far more animals into a limited space in battery houses or piggeries. But the 'big is beautiful' fashion is also stimulated by concessions, particularly the intervention schemes. These encourage farmers to go on producing as much as they possibly can in the sure knowledge that if they cannot sell their goods to the public, then the EEC will pay a good market price to put excess supplies into intervention stores. For example, when milk production reaches the point where stocks exceed demand, surplus amounts are bought off the market at an agreed price and the cost of the storage is met by the taxpayer. By November 1982, Britain, like the other EEC countries, had a growing surplus, estimated at 100,000 tonnes of milk powder in intervention.[15] Overproduction is now so ludicrously out of hand that estimates put the cost of running the intervention scheme at approximately £100 for every dairy cow in the EEC,[16] and there are more than 3 million dairy cows in the UK alone.

None of the various solutions advocated include the obvious one of discouraging farmers from overproduction by not paying them to overproduce. Instead, herd slaughter schemes have been introduced, by which dairy producers are invited to kill off their whole herd of perfectly healthy cows in return for a subsidy of approximately £400 per cow, plus up to a further £400 for the carcase. In the three schemes conducted since 1969, 2.2 million cows have been slaughtered at an estimated cost of over £500 million.[17] Yet at the end of it, there are still more dairy cows in the EEC than there were when the schemes began. Given these figures, our daily pinta begins to look a great deal more expensive than the price we pay for it.

Apart from leading to an early slaughter of millions of cows, this free licence granted to overproduction has other adverse effects upon animal welfare. As long as it remains profitable to overproduce, it is in the interest of farmers to keep as many animals as possible. Inevitably, this increases the likelihood of them adopting intensive systems. As we have seen, larger herds and higher-yielding cows present greater health problems; more cows mean more unwanted calves; this leads to an expansion of undesirable industries like the European veal trade, and subsequently an increase in the export of live animals from our own shores. It is another vicious circle of expanding violence.

Poultry farmers argue that they receive no similar incentives and it is true that ostensibly, they are not encouraged to overproduce to quite the same extent, since there is no existing intervention store for either chicken meat or eggs. But there is some financial support in other ways. Instead of storing eggs and poultry meat itself, the EEC encourages producers to dump the surplus elsewhere. Overproduction is made profitable by the export refund system, which allows farmers to sell excess products to third countries (usually in the Middle East and recently, North Africa) at a knock-down price in the secure knowledge that they will be able to reclaim most of the remainder of the EEC market price from Community funds. In 1981, £658,674[18] was paid out to Britain's poultry meat producers and a further £508,321[19] to their counterparts in the egg industry. In particular, egg producers are becoming increasingly dependent upon the export scheme to protect them against overproduction.

> A growing problem within the EEC is the steep increase in surplus egg production over the past six years, which is likely to continue next year. Egg exports to third countries have grown rapidly from about 1 per cent of production in 1976 to almost 3 per cent last year — around 20 million cases (30 eggs per case). A collapse of the export market for eggs would cause something close to chaos in the Community's egg market.[20]

(Those who would argue that this system helps those in poorer countries to eat eggs, are referred to chapter 8, 'The solution to world hunger'. There is no prospect of the poor obtaining these products).

*Pig Farming*, April 1983, states that the EEC is 'expected to double its subsidized export of eggs onto the international market during the 1982-83 period', yet still the poultry industry would have us believe that eggs could not be produced in sufficient quantity at a realistic price without battery cages. In fact, it is only because the same consumers who are supposed to benefit from cheap eggs are subsidizing the disposal of them elsewhere, that prices remain at current levels and the market is saved from a state of 'chaos'.

Alternatively, the egg industry directs its attention to other ways of getting rid of eggs at a decent price. The following statement, taken from a National Farmers' Union area journal, highlights the reality behind our so-called cheap food policy:

> As I write, the egg market is in a state of chaos. At present, there are too many producers giving away their eggs which is disrupting the whole market structure. I know of one

producer who sold his eggs to a wholesaler for 22p per dozen; the wholesaler took them straight round to the breaker and got 29p per dozen for them. When the situation in the egg market is like it is now, it is far better to sell your eggs to the breaker for 29p per dozen, than to let someone else take a profit out of you. By taking your surplus eggs off the market, you will be helping to strengthen trade.[21]

Here we see farmers encouraged to keep food off the market deliberately in order to stimulate prices. From the breaker, eggs go into almost every product imaginable, ranging from shampoo to plastics. Or absurd novel food products are invented, such as 'frozen omelette mix'.[22] Failing this, eggs are shipped about from country to country so that a flock of middle men employed in marketing and transport can make their own extra few pence and add a little to the retail price. For instance, it is difficult to know how the consumer is supposed to benefit from the fact that, in 1981, 34.6 million dozen eggs were exported from the UK to other EEC nations. At the same time, 32.3 million dozen were imported from the same countries![23] Moreover, on one publicized investigation into the export and import of eggs by the UK, it was discovered that one particular consignment was exported to Germany at 28.8p per dozen, where a Dutch dealer bought them and transported them to Holland. The *same* eggs were then sent to Belgium and finally re-imported to the UK at a cost of 34.8p per dozen![24] (No doubt at the end of their trip they were marketed as farm fresh!!)

Although such absolute idiocy is (hopefully) infrequent, the example illustrates the absurd principle of shipping perishable foods around from country to country when the same product can be obtained on the doorstep. It invites corruption, allows producers and dealers an extra bit of profit, and puts totally unnecessary additions on the retail price. Practised for the benefit of consumers? Nonsense. The more one goes into the problem, the more surely one comes to the conclusion that the abuse of animals in factory farming is only economic because of incentives which accompany it. What is striking about those incentives is their total representativeness of the economic strategies followed by the rest of society. That is, the bigger, more technologically complex and capital-intensive production methods become, the more 'economic' they are considered. It is no coincidence that these also happen to be the principles that most suit multinational business and financial investment.

Suppose that this pattern of 'aid' was altered in order to encourage the small rather than the big producer. What would happen if rate exemption was ended, or at least confined to those farmers utilizing acceptable welfare methods, with herd sizes not exceeding agreed numbers? What if factory farming was excluded from capital allowances on buildings and machinery on the grounds of public morality or rural protection? Since factory farming employs sophisticated machinery, this would save considerable amounts of money, which might possibly then be utilized on a grant encouraging greater use of labour. What would be the result if capital gains tax could only be avoided by farmers with a maximum of, say, 3,000 to 5,000 hens? What if there were no intervention stores or export refund systems available above an agreed excess, so that overproduction was actively discouraged?

If such changes were instigated, both battery production and massive farms would appear very much less profitable. This is not to oppose the principle that farming should be subsidized — in some circumstances it is right and proper to protect production — but rather to point out that when incentives give free licence to escalating violence to animals, the time has surely come to intervene and reconstruct the grant schemes to encourage more humane farming.

Are proposals for smaller flocks and herds, farmed less intensively, simply ridiculous? Would such ideas be disastrous to the farming community? Take the example of eggs once again: in 1982 out of 53,500 registered holdings with laying hens, 52,000 had fewer than 5,000 birds; 1,100 had between 5,000 and 20,000 birds; and there were only 400 holdings with more than 20,000 birds. Yet remarkably, these last housed 62.3 per cent of the national flock.[25] In the words of *Farmers' Weekly*, 'since these are likely to be the most capital-intensive, they would be the ones most affected by restrictions imposed upon the use of cages'.[26] These mammoth units also happen to constitute the majority of those owned by multinational interests. On the other hand, the cost of a changeover to non-battery production for the overwhelming number of holdings — 52,000 out of 53,600 — would not involve astronomical sums. In an ideal world, 5,000 hens in a unit is still far too many, but at least a reduction to that kind of size would be a move towards the kind of small flocks where animal individuality can be respected.

In response to such a suggestion, the poultry industry would doubtless claim that it would prove economically impossible to house the national flock in smaller units. In fact, such alternatives are perfectly feasible. Some countries have already encouraged such moves. In Switzerland, the small producer actually gets government help to keep down the size of his flock. As a result, 85 per cent of Switzerland's egg producers have less than 150 hens.[27] Conversely, the big producer is discouraged by a levy on every hen over 12,000.[28] In 1981, Switzerland also announced a 10 year rundown leading to a permanent ban on battery cages. Any method can be made 'economic' or uneconomic, according to the subsidies provided.

In the UK, Ministry of Agriculture figures put the total number of farms at 242,300.[29] If only one in four of these was to keep 1,000 hens, even the present-day mammoth national flock could still be housed satisfactorily.[30] Only 20 years ago (1961), 97 per cent of the country's laying hens were in units of less than 1,000; in 1969 the figure was still 85 per cent. In other words, massive flocks predominantly owned by non-farming interests is a recent phenomenon and not, as we are often led to believe, a long-established practice. It has grown over the last 20 years and there is no reason whatsoever why it should not be phased out even more quickly.

Objections to suggestions of smaller flocks and lower concentrations are easy to anticipate. For instance, what about the price of collecting and transporting eggs (or any other animal produce)? What about the cost of employing extra manpower? To take transport first, provided that we follow the principle that as much food as possible should be produced for local markets, the cost of transportation should, in fact, be reduced. Moreover, supplies for large cities could be met by farmers delivering to central collecting points in given areas. Whilst hard and fast rules are impossible to apply, and certain problems and expense are bound to be created, it is difficult to imagine that such a system would prove as uneconomic as the present one, where the same products are transferred to and from one European country to another, simply to adhere to economic theories of free trade between EEC countries.

As for the problems of employing extra labour to operate smaller, less intensive systems, former EEC Commissioner Dr Mansholt, offers an interesting insight into this problem:

> In farming, it would easily be possible to continue the smaller holdings with social aid. If three small farms of 15 hectares each are upgraded into one farm of 45 hectares, two families are out of work. As unemployment benefits amount to virtually 100 per cent of what the farm had been earning, society — that is all of us — must supply the wherewithal of these two families. But instead one could say: 'Let's leave all three of them on their 15 hectares and use the money to subsidize them.'
>
> Such policies become economically tenable. But they then represent large visible subsidies to agriculture from public funds, and at that point the Ministers of Finance get agitated.[31]

In this country, unemployment benefit does not quite amount to 100 per cent of what 'the farm had been earning'. Nevertheless, the principle expressed by Dr Mansholt is still applicable. To subsidize people to be 'gainfully employed' requires no additional financial outlay, merely different methods of distribution and support. On top of the money that could be switched from unemployment benefit in order to create jobs in agriculture, there could be comparative fortunes available from those subsidies which are at present paid out to encourage farms to become bigger and more intensive. Marion Shoard has estimated that each whole-and-part-time farmer in the UK is now supported 'to the tune of something like £8,500 per annum'.[32] In total, £5 billion is given to agricultural support every year. Admittedly, livestock farmers receive a smaller proportion of the total £5 billion given every year as subsidies to agriculture,[33] than others, but nevertheless, this massive figure illustrates clearly that when added to the policy of paying people to be employed out of the money put aside for unemployment benefits we could easily alter the support system in order to create opportunities for less violent farming.

Essentially, the enormous expansion of factory farming in recent decades has nothing to do with progress, economic need or inevitability. It is rather the result of big business using technological innovation in order to invade previously unexplored avenues for profit. This fact is demonstrated, for example, by the Imperial group. In 1969, the company realized that sales of their main source of income, tobacco, were likely to be badly affected during the following decade. Therefore, they examined the possibilities for alternative investment. Poultry seemed a suitable case for profit. Firstly they bought Ross Poultry and Ross Foods, paying £47 million.[34] Next, they purchased Allied Farm Foods, including Buxted Chicken and Nitrovit feed mills, for £19 million.[35] This deal gave them control of the biggest broiler chicken producers and one of the leading suppliers of animal feed to add to the Ross empire. Finally, they took over Eastwoods, the country's leading battery hen owners, for a sum of £39 million.[36] That made a total investment of £105 million. At the height of their domination of the poultry market, they owned approximately 115 million broiler chickens, 4 million turkeys and at least 20 million battery hens, as well as breeding and animal feed companies.[37]

In 1969, when Imperial first involved themselves in poultry production, 85 per cent of the national flock were in units of 1,000 or under. As Imperial and other 'giants' took greater control, however, units became bigger and bigger and the battery systems more dominant. The trends that had already begun in the previous decade accelerated alarmingly, coinciding with the enormous investment that multinationals could afford. Since 1961, the human population of the UK has increased by approximately 3 million; the poultry industry has increased out of all proportion — over 200 million more chickens, several million more hens and eight times as many turkeys. It is ludicrous to claim that this expansion is the result of economic necessity.

There is one crowning irony in all this. Despite all their cut-throat tactics, the multinationals are beginning to discover that factory farming is not quite as profitable as they had anticipated. After the initial quick profits in the 1960s and 1970s, mass animal exploitation is beginning to backfire. In March 1982, the Imperial group decided to cut their recent losses (£21.5 million in the previous two years) and get out of poultry production altogether. They sold their complete British interests to a firm called Hillsdown Holdings for £53.8 million, slightly more than half of what they paid for it![38]

This chapter has centred mainly upon poultry production, but the same argument is equally applicable to other methods of livestock production. Already, the pig industry is talking about 'the near-monopoly by the large companies in the pig-breeding industry'[39] — a state of affairs guaranteed to promote greater intensification along similar lines to poultry. It is simply untrue to suggest that these trends are being practised for the benefit of consumers. Rather, they are helping financiers to make quick profits, manipulating both animals and the agricultural support system in order to do so.

This second part of the book has attempted to discover 'the naked truth' behind the defences put forward for factory farming. Do not be fooled. Stripped of 'the rags of business verbiage and financial jargon'[40] battery farming is precisely what any disinterested observer spontaneously knows it to be. The 'naked truth'[41] is that it is a callous method of mass exploitation of animals practised for money. Is it not time to ring some changes?

# Part three

# Time for a change

# Introduction

Before any further discussion on how changes might be achieved, it is important to make one crucial distinction: that is, between action taken as individuals to fulfil personal convictions, and advancements which may be obtainable within the prevailing ethos of our civilization. As far as both animal welfare and world economics is concerned, near or total vegetarianism is the logical answer. Yet at the same time we must recognize that it is an answer that the majority of people are not yet ready to give. To hide ourselves away, self-righteously telling the world that it should not eat meat or even dairy produce may absolve our own consciences, but it is not going to improve the fate of many farm animals. A civilization accustomed to eating large amounts of animal protein is unlikely to be very impressed. Moreover, with agricultural economics now centred predominantly upon livestock farming, it is evident that any reduction in consumption of animal protein in the human diet is bound to be gradual.

Therefore, whilst working towards a long-term goal of devoting increasing areas of our land to the production of crops for direct human consumption, we must also put forward short-term policies aimed at significantly improving the living conditions for millions of farm animals and birds. Starting from the squalid mess we have now, we must suggest methods which at least enable animals to live some sort of natural life, without close confinement or other deprivation, before they reach the slaughterhouse.

Where to begin? First of all, compromises should not be taken too far. For example, even factory farms could be improved. Some are better than others. A dry-sow stall covered in straw is better than bare concrete; 6 inches of cage space in a battery is preferable to 4 inches. But to accept minimal changes such as a bit of bedding for pigs or an extra couple of inches of cage width for hens, would be an unacceptable compromise. Essentially, whatever is done to modify a cage or confinement stall, it is impossible to create an environment suitable to the needs of animals.

Before there can be any significant progress, factory farming must be abolished. It is useless to accept minor modifications; the rot goes far too deep. The bare minima to seek are living conditions for animals which at least demonstrate that we are travelling resolutely towards the ideal of non-violent agriculture. This means that all living creatures should be allowed space, exercise, comfort, companionship, freedom from mutilation, adequate light, food and water.

# 11. Alternatives

Even if we accept that both the present economic system and current levels of consumption of animal produce will continue more or less unabated, it is still possible to rear farm animals more humanely than at present. Alternative methods do exist, which are competitive financially and at least allow animals and birds to live out their short lives in environments which meet the majority of their most basic behavioural needs.

## Veal calves

Perhaps the most significant change has been to the modern system of keeping veal calves in straw-yards rather than in solitary crates. Significant, not only because it represents the most potent example so far of factory farming being replaced by a more acceptable method of production, but also because its adoption raises further doubts about the validity of the economic justifications for intensive practices.

Until recent years, veal calves were reared almost exclusively in crates on the grounds that there was no economic alternative. For example, a calf rearing supplement published in *Farmers' Weekly* in 1971, stated emphatically, 'Individual penning in a controlled environment building is one of two vital necessities for a big return on capital.'[1] In the following decade, however, public awareness of the unacceptable level of deprivation inflicted on calves in order to obtain the finished carcase, led to what was little short of a boycott of veal in this country. Faced with the choice of finding a more humane method of production or rapidly diminishing sales, it was not long before Britain's leading veal producers discovered the former. By 1980, Quantock Veal had destroyed all their veal crates and switched over entirely to straw-yards. In their own words, they did so because veal had become 'a dirty word' to the Britis

This development demonstrates conclusively the po
of public opinion. Admittedly, veal was never a particula.
food in this country and the sacrifice involved in the refus
chase was minimal. Nevertheless, it does suggest how quick͵ alternatives would present themselves if the public could be stirred to
similar action against other factory farmed products.

A still more encouraging feature of this breakthrough was Quantock Veal's announcement that the new straw-yard method is not only
more humane, but also more economic.[2] 'Individual penning and
controlled environment' which, according to the fashions of previous
years, had apparently been 'vitally necessary',[3] are now considered
both unnecessary and uneconomic by Britain's leading retailers. One
wonders whether similar results might be forthcoming from other sections of factory farming if abandonment of their methods was forced
upon the industry. Once livelihoods were threatened, how quickly
would the 'scientific experts' who tell us that there are no alternatives
to crates and cages, change their tune?

The straw-yard method of rearing calves for veal works roughly
as follows. Calves are kept in large, airy, covered barns, divided into groups of approximately 20 animals. Light and ventilation are both
natural, with shafts at the top of the barn and sliding panels at both
ends and along the sides allowing increased air-flow during favourable
weather. The concrete floor slopes gently forwards (1:20) with a 2ft
wide strip of expanded metal at the front for dung clearance. The
concrete floor is covered with a bed of straw. Outside each pen is
a machine which reconstitutes milk powder, heats the liquid food to
a suitably warm temperature and allows the calves to suck milk
whenever they want it from rubber teats inside the pen. Small quantities of iron are added to the feed to reduce anaemia.

From an animal welfare point of view the advantages of this
method over crates are self-explanatory. The calves have companionship, fresh air, light, enough room for exercise and play, can eat a
limited amount of their straw-bedding (thus allowing them to
ruminate), can lie down comfortably with access to a bedded area
and can suck milk whenever they want it. In addition, some animals
that were once killed at a few days old as 'bobby veal' can now be
satisfactorily 'raised on' under the Quantock method.

Of course, it is not a perfect system. No production of veal could be. Calves are still taken from their mothers near birth, killed at an early age and kept on a diet partly deficient in roughage. Nevertheless, relatively speaking, it is a humane way of rearing calves. At least, it represents a meritorious step in the direction of non-violence. At the 1981 Smithfield Show (the cup final of the meat trade) containing entrants from all over Europe, loose-housed calves won all the veal class awards for quality calves. Remarkably, however, the National Farmers' Union and the Ministry of Agriculture still refuse to push for a ban on the old crated methods. Consequently, both import and home production of crated calves continues.

## Egg production

Several alternative methods of large-scale egg production are already in commercial existence. All of them can be categorized roughly as improved versions of the deep-litter system that was particularly popular in the 1950s. Indeed, given good management and acceptable stocking densities, deep-litter itself can be a successful way of keeping large flocks.[4] Large units of more than 20,000 birds are possible, provided that the birds can be partitioned into groups that do not exceed about 750 and are allowed a minimum of 3ft per bird. The wide central area of the shed normally consists of a raised slatted floor above a dropping pit. This serves two purposes: as perches and dung collector. The two outside areas are covered with litter, usually straw. Against the walls, on both sides of the shed are rows of nesting boxes. Additional perches can also be added to make a more interesting environment. Although it is true that problems of aggression can be stimulated when the light is intense, successful farmers have overcome this by replacing fluorescent lights with bulbs; a change that does not diminish egg production. Farmers practising deep-litter systems can produce as many eggs as on any productive battery farm. Indeed, sample tests carried out by researchers at Zwolfte in Switzerland demonstrated that flocks on litter average 10 eggs per bird more than in batteries, with lower mortality rates. Examples of the breeds which showed better production figures on deep-litter are shown in Table 11.1. It is true that on the majority of deep-litter units, feed costs are likely to be higher during cold weather, though this

*Table 11.1* Comparison of egg production, deep-litter and battery cages

| Breed of hen | Hen housed average eggs/bird | | Mortality | |
| | Litter | Battery | Litter | Battery |
| --- | --- | --- | --- | --- |
| Lohmann LSL | 275.2 | 246.1 | 0.0 | 9.3 |
| Shaver 288 | 273.2 | 262.0 | 2.1 | 5.6 |
| Hisex White | 270.9 | 266.4 | 4.0 | 5.6 |
| Dekalb XI | 278.5 | 261.9 | 0.0 | 7.4 |
| Overall Average | 264.3 | 254.0 | 3.6 | 5.1 |

*Source*: *Poultry Industry*, 24, February 1983; figures taken from random samples at Zwolfte, Switzerland.

difference can be minimized by good insulation within the building. Feed and water can both be carried automatically to feed troughs within the building.

Types of straw-yard hen houses were popular in the 1930s, when birds were housed in open yards on a deep bed of litter. Unfortunately, when the weather was inhospitable, both the environment and the birds tended to turn into a squalid mess. In response to this problem, during the late 1970s at Cambridge University Faculty of Veterinary Medicine, Dr David Sainsbury developed covered straw-yards. Birds are kept in low-cost, covered barns, walled on three sides, but with the fourth side (normally facing south), fenced with wire to allow natural light and ventilation. There is no artificial heat or light, with the possible exception of an electric light on dark winter mornings, to stimulate egg laying. As with deep-litter, there is no problem with maintaining the levels of egg production. Dr Sainsbury obtains as many eggs from his straw-yard as from many commercial batteries.

The secret of the straw-yard's success is the deep bed of straw, approximately 1ft deep, which, remarkably, is changed only once a year, in summer. Provided that the house is kept dry, the combination of straw, droppings and fresh air, react bacterially to kill off any dangerous pathogens. In addition, the fermentation within the straw acts as an insulator to the hen house and helps to maintain the temperature. This ensures none of the reductions in winter laying normally associated with free-range. At Dr Sainsbury's unit, the litter remains so dry and clean that although the birds have been living on it for up to a year, it can be picked up and crumbled between the fingers without leaving any smell or mark.[5]

Straw-yards also have nesting boxes and perches to create a more 'natural' environment. In addition, the open fenced side encourages insects, thus giving the birds something to peck about for amongst the straw. Another interesting point is that even though the birds are moving about quite freely at a stocking density of about $3ft^2$ per bird, and therefore, using more energy than battery birds, they appear to consume slightly less protein food. This contradicts another of the ecomic defences for factory farming, namely, that by preventing animals from moving around one is reducing their energy output and consequently the amount of food they require. This 'time and motion' calculation is deficient in two ways. Firstly, it ignores the fact that birds are able to forage for some of their own food when unrestricted; and secondly, it fails to take into account that confined animals are inclined to eat partly out of boredom, as well as through hunger.

The Cambridge straw-yard consists only of a small flock of birds (250), with both feeding and egg collection carried out by hand. Provided hens are separated into groups of a similar size, there is no reason why large flocks with automatic feed should not be accommodated.

Many people believe that of all the alternatives to battery egg production, the aviary system is the most competitive. Once again, a covered barn with part litter and part slatted floor and nesting boxes on the inside of the outside walls of the shed is the basic principle. But whereas deep-litter and straw-yards use only the floor space of the house, aviaries, as the name implies, employ more than one tier and utilize the complete volume of the hen house. The obvious advantage is that this allows more birds to be housed in the same area. At the levels of stocking density being practised at the Ministry of Agriculture Experimental Aviary at Gleadthorpe, each bird is allowed $1ft^2$ of floor space. When this is converted to the whole volume of the shed, space allowance doubles to $2ft^2$ per bird. This allows comparative freedom. Birds move between the different levels by way of ladders, and these appear to provide considerable entertainment! At Martin Pitt's commercially successful aviary unit in Wiltshire, birds also have access to grassy outside runs, the extra space giving an overall stocking density of $3.5ft^2$ per hen.

Basically, aviaries consist of different levels, nests on all floors, food troughs, dunging areas, perches and a litter area. In several variations, the main preoccupation has been to plan in such a way as to keep the litter area as clean as possible. First-year trials by the Ministry at Gleadthorpe seem to have provided many well-publicized problems, but results have only been disastrous with certain strains of birds. For instance, Warren hens laid more eggs than the average battery unit (266) with similar mortality rates (6 per cent).[6] Whilst this may not represent an outstanding success, it is hardly the disaster that the farming press has been anxious to publicize. In addition, it must be stressed that the Gleadthorpe experiment has, so far, obtained results greatly inferior to both Martin Pitt[7] and research conducted in Europe at Celle, in West Germany.

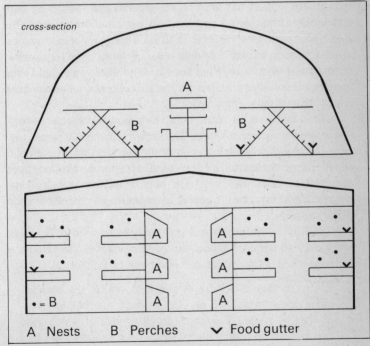

*Figure 11.1* The aviary system The diagrams show the aviary systems of two research projects. Above is the project carried out at Celle, West Germany; and below, at Laseur, in Holland.

*Source*: *Aktie Lekker Dier*, Holland, 1981.

None of these three alternatives is perfect; for instance, only in the straw-yards is natural light available. Nevertheless, all of them do at least allow birds to fulfil the majority of their behaviour patterns. They can perch, build up a social community, run, scratch, peck, flap their wings, walk, retire into a quiet corner when unwell, make dust-baths, live in a relatively varied environment and lay their eggs in a nest of their choice — none of these activities is available to the battery hen. Indeed, the most obvious examples of cruelty in cages, such as overcrowding, tend to overshadow the slightly more subtle deprivations such as the inaccessibility of nesting areas. On any system where choice is allowed, hens will spend significant periods sniffing around before choosing where to lay eggs; it is important to their natural instincts. Advocates of cages used to defend their failure to meet this need on the grounds that if hens lay their eggs in nests it presents a problem with dirty and broken eggs. But even if this argument was ever justified it has now been overcome by the invention of plastic nesting trays. Hens sit quite comfortably on these, and when the egg has been laid, it rolls down a slight slope to either a straw-filled container for manual collection, or an automatic belt if automation is employed.

There are two other semi-intensive systems which offer possible alternatives to factory systems. The Getaway cage is a larger cage than a battery cage, with lower stocking densities and an attempt to provide some interest for birds — sandboxes for dust-bathing, perches and nesting areas, etc.[8] On neither welfare nor economic grounds, however, does it appear as promising as the above mentioned methods.

The Pennsylvania system is apparently much used in Denmark, where only 40 per cent of hens are kept in batteries. The House of Commons Select Committee described this as follows:

Birds are housed on wire or slatted floors. In the commercial example which we saw in Denmark, the building was divided by a central passage, on either side of which were two large wire-netting enclosures each containing 900 birds at a density, excluding the passage area, of 14 per m$^2$ or 715 cm$^2$ per bird. Transverse beams about a metre from the ground supported a wire-mesh floor sloping 15 per cent through which the droppings passed to accumulate on the ground, whence they were cleared at the end of the laying cycle.[9]

Whilst clearly preferable to battery units, there are two major factors that make this system unsatisfactory as far as welfare is concerned. Firstly, the birds are rather too densely populated, and secondly, the environment is less interesting than other loose-house systems. In its present state, the Pennsylvania-style hen house does not offer a desirable alternative.

What of cost? Whenever this matter is discussed, the National Farmers' Union and the Ministry of Agriculture waste no time in publicizing the opinion that egg prices would double if cages are banned. Revealingly, however, they never offer any evidence to support these declarations. To be fair, it has to be admitted that with 96 per cent of eggs in this country now produced in cages, any attempt to assess accurately the costs of a changeover is difficult. Nevertheless, sufficient evidence exists to suggest that the actual increase in price to the consumer would be somewhere between 10 per cent and 15 per cent. Some facts:

1. In Holland, the Dutch Ministry of Agriculture runs a marketing scheme for non-battery eggs, known as *scharellei* (translated literally as 'scratching eggs').[10] To qualify for the premium paid out under this scheme, farmers must allow their hens litter on the hen house floor and stocking densities must not exceed 7 birds per m². The extra cost to the consumer is approximately 10 per cent.

2. In Switzerland, non-battery eggs are available at leading supermarkets alongside cage eggs. The extra cost is roughly 1p per egg. The Swiss marketing scheme is co-ordinated by the leading animal welfare society in the country, which also inspects farms.[11]

3. A report published by a commission studying alternative methods under the order of the Ministry of Agriculture in Holland, concluded 'that an egg from a battery is only ½p cheaper than eggs from a ground system'.[12]

4. In this country no such alternative marketing system exists. Indeed, some farmers producing eggs on litter systems are forced to sell their eggs to packers who mix them up with battery eggs.[13] The fact that they are able to do so offers further evidence that

differences in price need not be huge.

5. Perhaps the most revealing evidence of all is a desk study conducted by the Ministry of Agriculture's own advisory service in 1981.[14] The findings are shown in Table 11.2, indicating an estimated rise of 7p per dozen according to a Ministry whose sympathies are undeniably with the pro-battery lobby! Significantly, this survey does not take into account the most economic of the alternatives — aviaries. Professor Rose Wegner in charge of Europe's biggest poultry institute in Celle, West Germany, once a firm believer in the 'no economical alternatives to batteries' philosophy, recently announced that at Celle, aviaries are now fully competitive with batteries.[15]

*Table 11.2* Cost comparison of eggs from different methods of production

| Method of production | Estimated cost (pence per dozen) |
| --- | --- |
| Cages | 40.5 |
| Deep-Litter | 47.4 |
| Straw-yard | 47.4 |

6. After examining all available evidence, the House of Commons Select Committee concluded that a ban on batteries would result in 'an increase in price to the consumer of the order of 12½ per cent.[16] They added that 'it does not seem in itself an impossibly high price to pay to get rid of an undesirable system'. Surely many members of the public would agree with this, and be willing to pay that small extra cost to have the stamp of cruelty removed from the product?

These points show that batteries are unnecessary economically as well as indefensible on moral grounds. Indeed, when we compare the small fortune that has been spent on research into minimizing the cost of battery production compared to the paltry amounts that have subsidized investigations into the alternatives, one wonders what the results would be if the situation was reversed? Remembering the changes that have taken place in the veal industry, it is worth questioning whether aviaries and deep-litter might become *more* economic if large sums of money were invested in research into non-violence.

Whether or not this would be strictly true, we already possess ample evidence to announce a ban on battery cages within five years, as recommended by the House of Commons Select Committee. Realistically, such a time-span would be necessary in order to offset some of the financial costs of the changeover to more humane farming.

Believers in traditional animal farming methods will, by this time, wonder why no mention has been made of free-range egg production? It has to be admitted that whilst flocks remain so large, free-range does not offer much possibility of producing more than a small minority of the nation's egg supply. At an average stocking density of approximately 150 hens to an acre (to protect land from becoming fowl sick), it is obvious that large flocks are not feasible on many of our farms, although at least one producer in this country keeps over 6,000 birds on range. This is not to say that free-range egg production is a thing of the past. On the contrary, there is and will continue to be a growing demand for food from this traditional system. Producers employing either deep-litter with free-range grassy runs outside, or using the better-known method of keeping hens running around the farm as a 'side-line' for egg money, will multiply in order to meet the increasingly popular market. In addition, as indicated previously, once we reduce flocks to a more reasonable size, free-range becomes a more attractive proposition. It is worth repeating that if every farm in the country kept only 160 hens, we could still have an enormous national flock of almost 50 million hens.

The two main requirements for acceptable free-range egg production are sufficient land to keep free from fowl sickness (where flocks are relatively large, this would mean a rotation system), and well-insulated, weatherproof housing. Alternatively, the fold system can be employed, where hens are moved frequently around onto new strips of land. Moveable fences and housing are employed. This ensures both fresh pasture continuously for the birds and well-manured land for the next year's arable crops.

Without doubt the cost of completely free-range eggs is greater than under other systems. In the Ministry of Agriculture cost comparison, already mentioned, the estimated cost of production is 72.5p per dozen (79 per cent higher than in batteries). Many believe this figure is unrealistically high. In another study, conducted by Paul Carnell for Earth Resources, the extra amount was only 33 per cent.[17] In addition, a survey of 94 shops selling free-range eggs, carried out by the same person, showed that free-range eggs cost 30 per cent more outside London, and 45 per cent more inside London.[18] The actual cost of production was considerably less than this. Retailers paid only between 14 per cent and 24 per cent more than for battery eggs.[19] In Mr Carnell's own words, 'retailers' margins are substantially higher than for cage eggs'.[20] Naturally, this differential would diminish if cages were banned, because there would be far greater market competition. At present, free-range producers command an exceptionally high premium, precisely because demand far outweighs supply.

## Broiler chickens

It would be encouraging to be able to report similar alternatives to broiler chicken production. Alas, such systems do not exist. Although there are one or two large outdoor chicken farms on the continent, allowing birds to wander in woodlands and fields,[21] and a small number of enterprises which produce a few free-range chickens in Britain, almost all of the 370 million birds slaughtered annually in this country are broiler produced. Yet though we may be forced to concede that whilst such large quantities of poultry meat are consumed it seems inevitable that broiler farming will continue, this does not necessitate accepting the present situation. Improvement could be enforced within the broiler industry to ensure that concessions are made to welfare.

Many of the numerous health problems now associated with broiler chickens are the direct result of geneticists trying to breed birds that put on weight at an absurdly quick rate. Addressing the 1981 Poultry Industry Conference, Dr Colin Bracewell, from the Ministry of Agriculture's Central Veterinary Laboratory, had this to say:

> Leg disorders in broilers and turkeys now present a serious
> set of problems and everything that is being done by
> breeding, feeding and housing produces higher growth rates
> making the situation worse... Leg weakness also causes

financial loss at the production in terms of culls, and the humanitarian aspect needs to be considered carefully. It is difficult to accurately estimate the economic losses from leg disorders. One very crude figure, which is probably an underestimate, is the producers' culling rate from leg weakness plus the downgrading due to leg abnormalities of the processing plant. For broilers this probably lies between 3 per cent and 6 per cent.[22]

'Between 3 per cent and 6 per cent' of broiler chickens actually amounts to at least 1.2 million, and up to 2.4 million, birds. Although it is difficult to interest the poultry industry in 'humanitarianism' it appears that from an economic view alone, the endless pursuit of higher feed conversion growth rates may prove counterproductive. In answer to the problems he outlines, Mr Bracewell suggests that the industry should make 'a calculated, judicious reduction in growth rate' — a development which would also be welcomed by animal welfarists.

A second possibility for improved conditions for broiler birds is in the quality of their environment. At present, almost all birds are reared in controlled-environment sheds with both artificial light and heat. New developments in poultry house design, patented in Italy by Dr Agostino Volanti, now offer alternatives to conventional broiler houses, at least allowing natural ventilation and light. A few farmers in France, Spain, Belgium, Iraq, Saudi Arabia and the UK have now adopted systems based on Volanti's work. Dr Volanti's own unit is made out of greenhouse-type plastic, supported by steel and with an outer wall of black polythene. In between the plastic and polythene the shed is insulated with fibreglass. Ventilation and light are provided by inlets right down the length of the shed and in various parts of the ceiling. All ventilation shafts can be altered by a controlling handle.[23]

Other 'natural ventilation' broiler houses are in existence, using conventional wooden broiler sheds. The same principles apply: long ventilation shafts at the side and in the ceiling, inserted so as to ensure 'a steady flow of clean air without draughts, whilst maintaining an acceptable temperature'.[24]

As far as animal welfare is concerned, these open sheds have obvious advantages. A fresher, less dusty atmosphere gives 'improved results with quieter, better feathered flocks'.[25] Results so far also point to economic benefits. Building costs are about one-third less than in controlled broiler houses and no electricity is required for light, heat, fans or control panels. Provided that insulation is good, the sheds will remain sufficiently warm, even during winter.

The only economic drawback appears to be that 'slight reduction in stocking density'[26] is necessary. This, of course, is more than welcome to those concerned about the birds themselves. Present stocking densities in broiler sheds allow birds only $0.5ft^2$ each at slaughter weight. Increased space allowance, improved environment and slower rates of growth would at least ensure that birds would have the minimum of a meaningful existence before being slaughtered. Added perches would also improve the environmental conditions. In an industry committed to mass production of living creatures as if they were already lumps of meat on the dinner table, such changes would at least represent a step in the right direction.

## Pigs

In discussing possible alternatives in pig farming, we should be aware of three separate areas where current commercial practices are particularly unsatisfactory. These are: accommodation for breeding stock; farrowing and weaning arrangements; and the conditions for fattening pigs. Although much improved methods already exist for all three stages, it is surprising that some farmers may practise extensive farming for their breeding sows, whilst at the same time employing barren facilities for their weaners. What we shall be examining here is the best alternatives at all stages, beginning with traditional outdoor pig keeping.

A wide-ranging investigation conducted at Wye College, of the University of London, by Michael Boddington in 1971, concluded that 'pigs kept outdoors are in no way less profitable than those kept intensively'.[27] Although output of piglets per sow proved lower, this was more than compensated for by lower outlay on housing and mechanization. In Mr Boddington's own words, 'in the final analysis, the surplus achieved, however measured, compares more than favourably with the performance of the indoor herds'.

Despite these findings, almost all research and commercial development in the last decade has centred upon further intensification of indoor pig-keeping. Yet for all the investment into research, the relevance of the Wye College Report does not seem to have dated. On the contrary, judging by frequent articles in the farming press, the conclusions seem even more applicable today than they were in 1971. A special report in *Pig Farming*, July 1981, states that 'there now appears to be a distinct trend towards outdoor pig keeping in some parts of the country.'[28] Primarily, the reasons are economic: the initial capital costs are very much lower for an outdoor unit. Whilst it is true that there are tax concessions which favour factory farming after the initial cost of setting up a pig unit has been completed, the high original outlay for dry-sow stalls and farrowing quarters is prohibitive to small, independent farmers, unless they borrow huge sums from the bank. Generally, only the larger financial concerns are able to afford sophisticated intensive piggeries. Estimates put the capital requirements for the latter at £1,100 per sow compared to between £200 and £300 per sow for outdoor systems (this includes the cost of extra land).[29] The only equipment necessary outdoors are simple farrowing arks and fencing, compared to the complicated machinery and environmental control of dry-sow stalls, piggiboxes, and so on. Other advantages of the outdoor method include lower health risks and improved soil fertility where pigs are utilized as part of semi-arable rotation systems. Against this, the main financial reservations appear to be the extra use of land at a stocking density of an average 7-15 sows to an acre, and slightly lower levels of productivity. Figures supplied by the Meat and Livestock Commission for 1979 give the average number of piglets reared per sow outside at 18.5, compared to 19.1 indoors. Hardly a great difference.

Three other points should be made about outdoor pig-keeping. Firstly, the extra cost of land is partly reduced by the fact that poor quality soil can be utilized. Secondly, slightly more food is consumed by pigs on free-range (considerably more in winter, but less in summer when they can forage for some of their diet); and thirdly, it must be stressed that it is not a system suited to all areas. Quick-draining soil, preferably supported by a relatively dry climate, is essential. On water-retaining, heavy clay, the results of outdoor pig-keeping can be catastrophic. Fields can be turned to a muddy mess in a short period, making life miserable for both pigs and stockworkers.

Given these provisos (and also that there is sufficient space) sows normally build up a stable social order without many problems of aggression. Large numbers can be kept in undivided fields as long as there are regular water troughs to prevent one group of pigs having to cross into the territory of other groups. Also, feed piles must be spaced at sufficiently frequent intervals to avoid bullying. In other words, provided that the stockworkers and conditions are good, outdoor pig-keeping in an excellent system on both economic and welfare grounds, successfully practised by a growing minority of farmers.

Many outdoor pig farmers employ outdoor farrowing without losing any extra piglets. Although overall figures do show higher mortality rates where crates are not employed, there are certain breeds of pig well-suited to outdoor farrowing. Some are exceptionally careful mothers. With selected breeds and well-designed arks, mortality need be no higher outside. As one farmer remarked, 'When a sow gets in one of our huts and farrows it is as warm as toast in there, even on a bitterly cold morning. And we don't get a higher mortality rate among piglets in the winter.'[30]

From the point of view of the sows the major advantage of farrowing in unrestricted conditions is that she can fulfil all her maternal instincts. She can select material, choose a site and then carefully build her nest. After farrowing, some kind of fender is placed around the hut in order to prevent the piglets from leaving the ark for the first fortnight or so. The sow is left to suckle her young. At the end of the fortnight, the fender is removed and the piglets are left to follow their mother around the field.

Other outdoor farmers do employ farrowing crates. Sometimes portacabin-type buildings are taken to groups of sows who are then put into crates 24 hours or so before they give birth. Whilst this undoubtedly frustrates the sow's nest-building impulses, it is difficult to criticize those farmers who claim that they use crates because past experiences have taught them that piglet losses may be exceptionally high. At present, it is unrealistic to be dogmatic and to demand total abolition of crates. If sows are allowed bedding and returned to their arks not more than 72 hours after giving birth, it is at least much better than the increasingly common practice of keeping them in farrowing crates for up to 3 weeks. Nevertheless, we should look towards a time when crates are not used, since the intrusion on the sow's nesting behaviour and maternal instincts should not be underestimated. Indeed, some scientists go so far as to claim that the farrowing crate 'has a harmful effect... in cash as well as animal behaviour and welfare terms'. They argue that deprivation of nest building causes too much stress, as demonstrated by sows gnawing at the metal in their farrowing crate or pawing the ground in frustration. Commenting on investigations at the Scottish Farm Building Investigation Unit, Mike Baxter explains the theory as follows:

> This stress upsets the delicate hormonal balance which brings about labour and the birth process is protracted by uterine inertia. High levels of adrenalin caused by stress are known to block the hormone oxytocin which is so important to the farrowing sows. Reducing the hormone oxytocin prolongs and delays labour and this increases the number of stillbirths because the late arrivals are starved of oxygen.[31]

It remains to be seen whether Mike Baxter and his colleague, Carol Petherick, are proved correct in their theory. What does seem clear is that even where farrowing crates are employed, there is no need to keep the sow crated for 2-3 weeks after the birth of piglets. To do so is wholly for the convenience of the stockworker; not for the benefit of the sow, nor for saving the lives of the young.

On acceptable outdoor units, piglets can run with their mothers for at least 5 weeks and a maximum of 8 weeks, after which they are moved into fattening quarters. Some farmers only breed pigs and sell the young off to other farmers for fattening. Contradicting modern trends, a recent study at the Scottish Farm Buildings Investigation Unit concluded that 5-week weaning is more profitable than the increasingly popular practice on factory farms of weaning at 3 weeks.[32]

Not all fattening quarters include the all too common deficiencies of inadequate space, light, floor materials, dunging area and also lack of bedding. Perhaps the best system is where pigs are reared up to slaughter weight in roomy, airy, cattle-type buildings on straw bedding, with long feeding troughs across the house going some way towards minimizing aggression at feeding time. Apart from bedding and feed arrangements, space is particularly important in all fatten-

ing quarters. The new Codes of Practice for pigs suggest only 5.5ft²
for pigs weighing 100lbs.[33]

What about indoor units? Although outdoor pig keeping is the
most desirable method, it would be a mistake to condemn all indoor
units. Some are far better suited to the natural life of the pig than
the most intensive piggeries. Although there are a diversity of practices employed indoors, the better systems usually work along similar
principles. Small groups of sows are housed together throughout their
pregnancies. The typical unit would consist of sows divided into
groups of about 6, with a reasonably large straw-covered living area.
From here, an open doorway would lead to a much smaller living
place, together with a dunging area. Beyond this would be individual
feeding stalls, into which each sow would be shut at feeding time to
avoid bullying. The dunging area is normally placed in line with the
outdoor side of the shed, so that a tractor can easily go down the whole
length for clearance (see Figure 11.2).

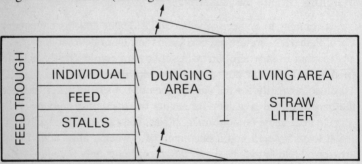

*Figure 11.2* Indoor pig unit

Problems of aggression can be mostly overcome, because any sow
under attack can retire behind the corner of the living area, out of
sight of would-be aggressors.

The traditional multiple suckling unit is another method allowing pigs some degree of natural life before slaughter. Groups of sows
are housed together in straw-yards, sometimes with an outside run.
Sows and their litters live together in the yards until the young are
weaned.

Even in research establishments, protests against factory farming of pigs are beginning to take effect. Some scientists are now

carrying out admirable work in an attempt to fit the environment to the needs of the pig, rather than vice versa. Particularly interesting in this respect is the work undertaken at Edinburgh School of Agriculture by Dr David Wood-Gush and Dr Alex Stobla.[34] They began by observing the behaviour of a group of sows left unrestricted in a varied natural environment. They observed that pigs had a stable social order, a daily routine, and showed considerable enterprise. From these studies, the two doctors then attempted to produce an indoor system which, at the very least, would allow the pigs some opportunity to express their natures. The result is a further improvement over the indoor methods described above.

Pigs live in family houses. Firstly, four in-season sows are kept together in a pen with a boar. After mating, the boar is moved on to another group of sows, whilst the females remain together throughout their pregnancies. Bales of straw are left in a farrowing area and the sows are left to choose and build their own nests. After farrowing, sows tend to feed only their own young, using areas well clear of their pen-mates. Then, whilst the mother pig is still lactating, the boar is re-introduced into the pen. This is 4-8 weeks after farrowing. Lack of stress in the family pen encourages the sow to accept the boar in this period, even though she is still feeding young. Her litter then stay in the family pen until slaughter weight is reached, which is usually before the sow is next due to give birth.

The advantages of this family pen are self-explanatory. Mating, farrowing, weaning and social grouping are all to a large extent centred around the animal's natural life cycle. Moreover, there are environmental advantages. As well as the farrowing area, living quarters, feeding stalls and dunging area, there is a recreation area included to answer the pigs' need for exploration. Rubbing posts, logs and small pieces of timber, rooting areas with peat and water troughs are all found in this area to provide an interesting environment (though they do not as yet go as far as wallowing areas).

Dr Wood-Gush and Dr Stobla do not anticipate that the family pens will prove particularly expensive. They estimate that each sow and family requires 300ft$^2$, compared to 175ft$^2$ under the more intensive systems. The reasons why the difference is relatively small is that all the families are contained within the pen; no room is wasted with passages to move pigs from (say) stalls to farrowing pens or farrowing pens to fattening quarters. They also believe that the family pen would prove advantageous to pig health because there are none of the hazards created by moving pigs from place to place and introducing them to new groups. As an indication of the stress-free state of the young pigs, the doctors have stated that they have not had to dock the tails of any piglets.

The family pen is not yet in commercial existence. Nevertheless, it represents exactly the kind of enterprise that can reverse the trend of ever-increasing violence in agriculture. Hopefully, it will soon be developed sufficiently to be introduced on to farms.

## Dairy farming

As far as dairy farming is concerned, there is not so much question of suggesting alternative methods because, in essence, the system of grazing outside in summer and spending the winter months in indoor barns is suitable to the needs of the animals involved. Having said that, dairy farming is still stepping along the same path of violence as other forms of intensive livestock keeping. To reverse this trend, we need, above all, to abolish the fashion for bigger and bigger herds, because of the inevitable welfare problems that accompany them. Unless we do so, zero-grazing herds of hundreds of cows kept 'knee deep in slurry cubicles' may increase, bringing greater problems with mastitis and other environmental diseases. As a rule, smaller enterprises have fewer problems of lack of space, lack of adequate bedding and infrequent mucking out. Consequently, there is less pressure on farmers to introduce bare concrete or other unsatisfactory flooring arrangements into their cowsheds.

The obsession with higher-yielding cows also needs to be shown up for the needless abuse of animals which it actually is. The mad rush to get heifers into calf earlier and earlier; the transference of embryos from productive to less economic cows; milking cows three times a day; genetic breeding resulting in cows with udders swinging near the ground; the race to separate cow from calf and get the mother back into calf again: why do we need these practices? It is nothing more than worship of technology for technology's sake on the one hand and profiteering on the other. Exemplifying the former, we quote Alick Buchanan-Smith, the Minister of State for the Ministry of

Agriculture, addressing the Oxford conference on farming at the beginning of 1981. His subject was 'Agriculture's role in Britain's recovery'.

> As a result of advances in breeding and management we have seen average yields per cow rise from 3,000 litres in the early 1950s to around 4,700 litres, today. In the Dairy Management Scheme last year, the top 25 per cent of herds hit an average of almost 6,000 litres — plenty of scope there for the national average to improve further still...
>
> What I find exciting is not simply that as one technology becomes further developed — perhaps towards the point of diminishing benefit — another appears; it is also that each new technology appears to reach commercial exploitation even more swiftly than the last.
>
> Take, for example, embryo transfer. The ARC units at Cambridge carried out the first successful transfer of a bovine embryo, which was first frozen then thawed, in 1972. Only eight years later this is now an established commercial practice, and we are just on the threshold of what may be achieved in livestock improvement by these means.

Mr Buchanan-Smith does not question where these technological achievements are leading. The cost to the cattle, milk surpluses of astronomical proportions and the subsequent cost to the taxpayer (who pays for the original research into higher-yielding cows, intervention stores and finally, more research to discover possible novel markets to mop up the milk lakes!!), are all conveniently ignored. The search for higher milk yields represents another example of animals being made to suffer for no greater purpose than humanity's conceit and greed. Whilst it is impossible to make dairy farming completely humane, we could surely work towards the ideal by encouraging small herds kept in comfortable winter housing, allowed to mate, calve naturally and suckle their young, if only for a short period. To do so might mean less milk, but in a community with a surplus of millions of tonnes of milk powder that might not be a bad idea.

## Conclusion

As a final point, it must be stressed that humane farming does not necessarily mean putting the clock back and returning to traditional methods. Every year between 1 million and 3 million new-born lambs die, mainly from hunger and exposure.[35] The financial loss is estimated at £28 million a year.[36] What could be more humane and economic than to try and defeat this suffering by promoting indoor lambing in straw-filled barns or even complete overwintering of flocks of ewes when the weather is severe? Intensive farming where animals also benefit is one thing; it is application of intensive principles solely for profit, convenience or to display technological ingenuity that is to be condemned and defeated.

It has to be admitted that some of these improved conditions demand higher standards from stockworkers than battery farming. One may go further and add that a humane system badly managed may result in more intense physical suffering for animals than a factory farm operated negligently. But to say this does not justify the latter. Until we create conditions where farm animals at least live in comparative freedom, there cannot be any moral argument for keeping livestock at all.

From examples quoted here it is evident that it is not even necessary to disturb current food habits or economic systems in order to make a start in creating some kind of improved balance between the needs of farm animals and the profit motive. We can abandon the more ruthless forms of exploitation without an enormous upheaval; only the political will to make a positive stand is required. Hopefully, once the first steps towards non-violent agriculture have been taken we may be sufficiently encouraged to pursue that worthy goal further.

# 12. Small is preferable

Our investigation of factory farming and the forces dictating it has pinpointed several characteristics irreconcilable with animal welfare. Apart from the methods themselves, the main problem is that the scale of operations is altogether too large. Too many animals are being reared, transported and slaughtered, animals are being transported too far; farms themselves are too big and too capital-intensive; vested interests have too much money-power and so on.

As long as this trend towards greater concentration continues then the obstacles against non-violent agriculture remain insurmountable. Whilst the meat and poultry trades demand anything approaching the same mass killing of huge numbers of animals, there remains little prospect of achieving even relatively humane transport and slaughter, and to a large extent this invalidates many of the improvements that could be introduced in the rearing of animals.

Of course, action could also be taken to reduce suffering between leaving the farm and completion of the slaughter process. Environmentally controlled lorries for poultry transport; further reductions in the permitted maximum journeys between farm and abattoir; better designed slaughterhouses; improved stunning and slaughter equipment; training courses for slaughterers and handlers; stricter enforcement of the servicing of equipment; abandonment of piecework rates: these are only a few of the areas where changes need to be made. Indeed, a whole chapter could be devoted to discussing many improvements which would at least reduce the levels of suffering endured by animals at the end of their lives. But to do so would be to miss the essential point that progress in these areas would have only a comparatively minimal impact whilst the blood continues to flow at such a rate.

The only answer is to drastically reduce our intake of animal produce. Not only for the sake of our farm animals, but also in response to the 500 million members of our own race who are starving. We cannot afford to feed more high-protein foods to imprisoned animals, any more than we can affort to brutalize our own sensibilities by treating sentient creatures as if they were no more than 'sticks or stones'.

We have now reached the point where, according to *Poultry World*, in 1981 'poultry and egg producers were customers for 50 per cent of cereal produced in Britain'.[1] This situation is ludicrous. Until we alter our own policies and begin to grow more vegetable protein for direct human consumption, demonstrating to poorer nations an agricultural policy worthy of imitation in both its rational use of resources and its sensitive treatment of the land and other living creatures, we can make no meaningful contribution towards alleviating hunger in the world.

Unfortunately, the basic questions remain. How can those with power be persuaded to introduce policies which take into account both moral values and long-term economic consequences? How can governments be pressurized into action? More specifically, what sort of viable policies should they introduce?

Let us consider the last question first. Primarily, of course, we should wish to secure radical changes in animal welfare legislation itself. The particular practices that need to be outlawed, and some possible alternatives, have already been discussed in previous chapters: basically, we are looking for living conditions which allow animals to live a life natural to each individual species; minimal journeys to slaughterhouses; and a death as quick and painless as possible.

But it will take much more than legislation on farm animal welfare to initiate any deep-rooted change in our civilization's response to the problems of food production. Beliefs, attitudes and political policies all have to be attacked at a more radical level. Therefore, a few issues are discussed here which, whilst not always directly involved with animal welfare, do, nevertheless, have an important bearing upon the possibility of a less violent future.

One obvious way of promoting more sensible agricultural policies would be through tighter controls over the money spent on research. In 1980-81, £33 million was given over to research on farm animals, most of it geared solely towards increasing production,[2] (i.e. more profit). Work included in this category is transferring goats' udders to their necks, earlier weaning of piglets, multiple births in lambs, and further research on embryotomy in cattle. All such work should be curtailed. As soon as we switch our priorities from maximizing animal production, to feeding people adequately and treating animals more humanely, then we can see these examples of extreme abuse for what they actually are: worthless. In fact, the only research involving farm animals which is justifiable is where the aim is either to provide a richer living environment or to reduce suffering. Two examples in this category which come to mind are the work with pigs in family pens at Edinburgh, and the attempt to demonstrate the economic disadvantages of farrowing crates (both discussed in chapter 11).

More than this, however, we must, in future, recognize that research with farm animals is of secondary importance compared to the further development of vegetable proteins. We need to investigate widely the possibilities of growing new varieties of pulses, seeds and grains on our land and also promote the technology to utilize their protein value. For instance, an acre of land devoted to lucerne, sunflower, soya, field beans, clover, lupins, field peas, or nut trees will produce far more protein per acre than any form of animal production. All of these (with the exception of soya where there remain problems with obtaining a variety suitable to our climate) can be grown in this country and offer considerable potential as sources of human food. In particular, the white lupin seems to offer great promise as a source of vegetable protein. Eminently suited to our climate and soils, and easily harvested, research has shown 'that in most respects sweet lupin seed approaches equivalence to the soya bean as a protein supplement'.[3] In fact, there is nothing new or faddish about the use of white lupins in the human diet: evidence points to the fact that the Egyptians utilized them as early as 2000 BC.[4] They also have potential as a source of famine-relief food. A water-soluble pellet consisting of 70 per cent wheat and 30 per cent lupin seed meal has been produced in Australia, is easily stored and offers a 'nutritionally balanced food for emergency feeding of a population following natural disaster'.[5]

With food technology, many 'novel' crops could be processed into a range of nutritionally valuable products. (By processed, we mean a similar process to the way we obtain wholemeal bread from wheat and not the kind of process often employed by commercial enterprises, involving the extraction of food value from the original crop.) Development of these foods does not mean that we should abandon our traditional sources of vegetables and grains. On the contrary, agricultural scientists should be encouraged to develop as wide a range as is practicable of nutritious and flavoursome foods.

At present, these ideas are not as widely supported by government as they deserve to be. For instance, it was significant that one of the first research spending cuts made after Mrs Thatcher's government came to power was at the Scottish Plant Breeding Organization, effectively curtailing their work with the latest developments on cultivation of oats. Such a decision typifies the shortsightedness that needs to be opposed. Simply because oats are a relatively unimportant part of our diet at present it does not mean that some time in the future we will not be grateful for all available knowledge about this versatile and nutritious cereal, which can provide food for humans in a variety of forms such as porridge, rissoles, cakes, etc. Responding to the financial cuts, the director of the station, Dr Macer, made the following pertinent statement:

> We should be attempting to develop a more diverse range of crop plants. We should also be searching for plants capable of producing high yields with lower requirement for high energy-demanding inputs (for example nitrogen) and developing the cultural practices to exploit such material.[6]

Undoubtedly, a reduction in our dependence upon animals would be one effect of a 'more diverse range of crop plants' which would demand lower energy inputs, reducing the strain on the world's energy resources. An educational programme may be necessary, stressing the cultural advantages of modifying our diets in order to accommodate new crop plants.

This leads us inevitably to the question of how we can 'develop the cultural practices to exploit such material'. How are we to set about changing from a society addicted to animal-based convenience foods, to a more independent and food-conscious population? How do we promote awareness of both the limitations of world resources and the full range of potential alternatives in our diet? Obviously, a mammoth educational effort is necessary, particularly in schools. Ultimately, no children should leave school without being able to provide themselves with tasty and nutritional meals and without always basing them upon animal produce. Home economics must become a subject of increasing importance, educating children to the numerous problems that exist in world food production and encouraging responsible attitudes in the battle to alleviate them.

Apart from a practical demonstration of nutritional alternatives, we need also to show our young people precisely what is involved in bringing them their foods. Let us admit freely the degree of violence involved in animal production. By contrast, our present attitude is to do everything within our power to disguise the relation between dead animals and the food on our plates. So much so, that we allow commercial interests to utilize both advertising and 'educational' material showing happy smiling, caricature chickens and pigs,[7] almost implying that animals are joyously awaiting their trip to the slaughterhouse! Surely it would be more educationally valuable to make children think about the ways in which their dinner is produced, rather than for them to accept passively whatever greets them on the supermarket shelf or dinner plate. Other kinds of propaganda from commercial companies are equally misleading. For instance, in *Shell Education News*, we find an article entitled 'Why farmers need chemicals'.

> By the year 2000, it is estimated that the world will need another 50 million tonnes of meat per year, another 100 million tonnes of milk, as well as vast cereal, sugar and vegetable requirements. Animal husbandry methods will have to improve considerably — and the use of chemicals to control parasites and disease in animals must increase.[8]

The truth behind statements like 'the world will need another 50 million tonnes of meat per year' and 'the use of chemicals... must increase' is that these trends are necessary only to ensure that companies with vested interests continue to make profits. On no other grounds do we need more meat or 'improved animal husbandry methods'. (Heaven knows what atrocities to animals this might include!) On the contrary, nothing could be further from our real needs.

The aim of such an educational programme would not be to turn all children vegetarian overnight, nor to tell them that this diet is right or that diet is wrong. On the contrary, the object should be to make children aware of every possible choice, from factory farming to less intensive farming; from less reliance on animal protein through to vegetarianism and veganism. They should hear the case for and against all systems and also be offered the practical skills which would enable them to live according to their beliefs as soon as economic independence has been attained.

No doubt it will be argued that a school curriculum already overcrowded with examination studies can ill-afford the time to indulge in such a 'minority issue' as the way we use the land to bring us our food, or our attitude towards the creatures with whom we share the planet. In response, one can only suggest that if this is so, we may well have our priorities hopelessly wrong, particularly at a time when human hunger is on the increase and energy resources are dwindling. Moreover, is it not rather a contradiction that a society priding itself on greater educational opportunities for all has in fact, produced a population where fewer people have any awareness of how their food reaches them than ever before? More and more, our population relies upon convenience products brought to them almost exclusively by a few giant companies.

Obviously, as cities get bigger and people continue to lose contact with the country, so the task of reversing current trends becomes increasingly difficult. An enormous conscious effort is required. Many children in cities have never even seen a farm animal, as reported by one East London teacher, who, when she asked one of her pupils to draw a chicken, found herself confronted with a picture of a dressed and cooked carcase! Respect for animals is unlikely to blossom out of such ignorance. For this reason, provision of well-run city farms, where children can mix with animals and discover that they are responsive creatures with their own individuality, seems wholly worthy of support.

In addition, wherever possible, vegetable plots should be provided at schools for pupils to learn about the soil and vegetable growing, as well as allotments for all those members of the adult population who require them. The possible benefits of such provisions should not be underestimated. For many people, watching and helping things grow offers emotional and spiritual satisfaction, as well as economic advantages. Whilst economic gains are not necessarily the prime reason we wish to provide as many vegetable plots as is humanly possible, it is worth adding that they could also make a significant contribution towards the nation's food production. In *Energy and Food Production*, Gerald Leech draws attention to one unpublished survey, revealing the following:

> In 1951, Best and Ward made a study of 600 gardens in London suburbs. They found, to everyone's surprise, that the financial output of food per unit area for the average house and garden plot was very close to that for the best farmland. (£42 and £45 respectively) and substantially higher than for average farmland (£36 per acre). Since on average only 14 per cent of home-plot area was actually used for growing fruit and vegetables, the difference is remarkable.[9]

Old though these figures may be, Leech's purpose in quoting them it to illustrate their continuing significance. They point to the economic value of garden plots in a rational system of agriculture in that they can help greatly towards self-sufficiency. This is not to claim that all individuals want to grow their own food, nor that pressure should be put upon them to do so. It is rather to demonstrate that what might first appear a minor contribution towards our economy, may, if encouraged, prove quite significant. There is, in fact, plenty of unused land available. There are at least 250,000 acres dormant land in urban and industrial areas alone.[10] Even allowing for more housing and industrial developments, good planning could surely create many more allotment areas? This example also illustrates how small-scale food production is always more efficient than large-scale (contrary to all modern trends) because the land tends to be used more carefully. Let us do all that we can to ensure that the growing numbers of people who would like to become more involved in food production are given opportunity to fulfil this desire.

None of the examples suggested will bring about immediate change. Indeed, their overall effect may be limited. Nor are these ideas intended to offer a complete programme of reform. Rather, they represent more or less symbolic examples of the kind of direction we need to take. If implemented, they might hopefully promote some feeling and respect for the land and its creatures.

At the same time as we take action to encourage small-scale food production, governments should also take corresponding steps to discourage the massive enterprises which now dominate our agriculture. To achieve this end will involve a courage rarely observed in the narrow world of party politics. Basically, what is required is what amounts to legislation against multinational interests, as opposed to the hand-in-glove policies that governments tend to adopt towards them at present. This action is necessary because as long as uninhibited movement of capital remains permissible, there can be no limit to the size of investment in agriculture. This state of affairs more or less ensures the perpetuation of exactly what we have now — mammoth farms with too many animals and large investment in machinery to the exclusion of manpower. Quite frankly, not until legislation is introduced in order to inhibit multinationals can there be any way of reducing the influences which have been primarily responsible for the alarming escalation of factory farming. Whilst those same forces sustain control, the result will almost certainly be more animal suffering, more food wastage, less jobs, and greater control of food production in the hands of a small number of companies.

Nowadays, any suggestion of introducing controls over the free market economy will, inevitably, be greeted with derision and accusations of 'communist propoganda' and 'anti-democratic'. In fact, nothing could be further from the truth. It is a belief held widely by a whole range of thinking people, some of whom it would be ludicrous to accuse of communist sympathies. Amongst the most notable is Dr Siccio Mansholt, who, as mentioned previously, was formerly EEC Commissioner and Dutch Minister of Agriculture:

> It is safe to say that the free movement of capital always leads towards concentration. This makes it possible to obtain the largest possible profit at relatively low risk. Capital does not favour small units...
>
> At the time when there were still unlimited opportunities for expansion, the free market economy was unquestionably very successful in raising the standard of living and increasing expansion. But we are entering a new social order. These times will not return. Once you come to this conclusion, you will have to minimize growth. We shall need to

have smaller enterprises on a recycling basis — concentration as we know it cannot go on — then we must have the guts to develop policies which control capital. Free market economy is inconsistent with development towards a society composed of small production units.[11]

When questioned further as to whether his suggestion 'to develop policies which control capital' are 'contrary to genuine democracy', Dr Mansholt offers the following pertinent remark:

Self-reliance of people is an important part of real democracy. Parliamentary democracy without a self-reliant people, both at work and in other facets of life, is not true democracy. Democracy is more than casting your vote once every four years... One may well say that strong concentration into mammoth concerns is anti-democratic.[12]

As Dr Mansholt intimates, there is no true democracy in a system of food production dominated by a few companies with more money than everybody else. This is particularly so when the dominant forces act in a manner that can best be described as anti-social — as in the case of factory farming.

By contrast, the few suggestions put forward here at least work towards a democratic system where more people have greater opportunity to think about and participate in the production of their own food. Undoubtedly, this would result in the abandonment of factory farming.

# 13. Taking action

The task is massive; the forces working against abandoment of factory farming and all the values that it stands for are formidable. Let us freely admit that if we are to create a world which puts animals before profit, long-term consequences before short-term greed, or life before balance sheets, it requires nothing short of a revolution in human attitudes. As a result, the temptation amongst the many individuals appalled by the sophisticated barbarism of factory farming is to lapse into despondency or bitter cynicism. Understandable as such a reaction is, however, it helps nobody but the vested interests. It is playing right into their hands. We must remember that only through individuals working tirelessly to convince other individuals do insignificant minorities develop into influential pressure groups. The seeds of revolution can only be sown in individual human hearts. No doubt opponents of other social evils throughout history, from the anti-slavery movement through to the fight for womens' rights, felt similar alienation and helplessness in the early days of their campaign; and who would have thought that Gandhi's policies of civil disobedience through active non-violence could have freed India? There are hopeful parallels in the past and there are already hopeful signs now, as increasing numbers of people devote their spare time, energy and money to this cause in which there is no personal profit. The meat and poultry industries are worried. Conference after conference and expert after expert are being summoned in an attempt to convince the public that there is no alternative to factory farming. But it is not possible to satisfactorily defend the indefensible. The arguments are becoming more extreme and more transparent, culminating in the kind of hysteria displayed in the following quotation from *Poultry World*. The writer is discussing campaigners against factory farming.

With no wars to fight, empire to rule or natives to save, the militant missionaries who want to turn back the clock seem well on their way to winning, at least the battle of words.

If I refer to them as a sort of pseudo-intellectual middle-class National Front it is not in order to insult, but to underline their approach, their attitudes and background. Not for them the commercial world, merely the cosy academic process of thought and talk without consequence, with views then paraded that are designed to overturn the established order.

The same people go to endless trouble to save whales, stop the building of nuclear power plants and as a recent investigation in a national newspaper appears to confirm, have a common left-wing link that would have us disarmed in a moment given the chance.[1]

Basically, there are two ways in which we can fight for change: collectively and individually. Collectively, we can form ourselves into organized local groups with the common aim of spreading public awareness and keeping the issues constantly in the news. These groups can be both affiliated to the relevent animal welfare societies and independent enough to initiate their own local activities. Above all else, it is vital to get out onto the streets and distribute literature. Apart from leaflets (which the national societies will provide) all that is needed is reasonable display material plus hard work and determination. In addition groups can write constantly to the media, establish contact with the local press, organize public meetings, contact local schools, raise funds, compile lists of free-range producers, make local MPs aware that some people are prepared to vote across party lines for the candidate prepared to fight for improved legislation for animals, and so on. Generally it is a case of everybody doing what they can, where they can, depending largely upon the talents within each group.

As well as campaigning collectively, one can also influence others a great deal by individual efforts. Try to boycott all factory-farmed produce. In addition, allocate at least two meatless days in recognition of both the extent of animal suffering and the problems of human hunger. Invite friends to share your meatless days, thereby spreading awareness of the nutritonal advantages of non-meat meals. Use every opportunity to contest the need or moral acceptability of factory farming.

As soon as they learn what is involved in the production of food from animals, many people become convinced that the only alternative to farm animal cruelty is vegetarianism. Vegetarians argue that whether or not we improve living conditions for our livestock, we remain confronted with the unavoidable violence of the slaughter of young and vigorous creatures for food that we do not need. Until recently, vegetarianism has had rather a 'cranky' image, even though its advocates in the past have ranged from Pythagoras, Socrates and Leonardo da Vinci, through to Milton, Voltaire, Shelley, Wordsworth, Tolstoy, Shaw and Gandhi. Nowadays times are changing and vegetarinism is very much more accepted.

Veganism is also gaining in popularity. Vegans eschew all animal produce, including dairy foods. To put it as simply as possible, the central argument is that whilst the consumption of milk, cheese, eggs and butter does not necessarily involve immediate cruelty to animals, it is indirectly responsible for considerable misery. The early separation of young from mother; the problem of what to do with the surplus calves; the fate of 'barren' cows discarded to the slaughterhouse after their usefulness is over; unwanted male chicks destroyed at a day old: these are a few of the unanswerable difficulties that lead increasing numbers of people to turn to a diet which avoids totally any food that has passed through animals. Vegans also point to the possible economic, ecological and health advantages of food production based mainly upon pulses, seeds, nuts, fruits, grains and vegetables.

Other than to stress the need for a reduction in meat eating, the aim of this book has not been to tell people how to live their lives. Rather, there has been an attempt only to put forward the facts about what is involved in modern animal production for both animals and people; to show how current trends can only become more extreme whilst we maintain the same principles; and, by contrast, to outline a few of the possibilities for a different kind of future. A list of names and addresses is included in the appendix for all those interested in pursuing further some of the alternatives suggested. All that is needed is a real consideration of the misery and squalor of battery cages, poultry transportation or dry-sow stalls, and action in whatever way seems appropriate. *Everybody* has something to contribute.

# Notes

## 1. Poultry

1. Ministry of Agriculture statistics. All Ministry figures quoted are prepared by Government Statistical Service.
2. *Ibid*.
3. For a description of deep-litter systems see chapter 11.
4. Ministry of Agriculture statistics.
5. *The Poultry Industry*, the Imperial group information brochure. Imperial group 1974.
6. W. Jaksch, 'Euthanasia of day-old male chicks in the poultry industry', *International Journal of Studies in Animal Problems*, vol.2, no.4, 1981.
7. Ministry of Agriculture statistics.
8. *The Poultry Industry*.
9. Ministry of Agriculture letter to Compassion in World Farming, 29 June 1978.
10. Proposals put forward at a meeting of the EEC Council of Agriculture Ministers, 30 March 1983.
11. 'Beware of units with more than 80,000 layers', *Poultry World*, 10 June 1982.
12. Ministry of Agriculture letter to Chickens' Lib, December 1982. The NFU estimate is quoted from 'Would you vote for Animal Lib?', *Woman's Own*, 19 February 1983.
13. Ministry of Agriculture letter to Mrs D.E. Amey, 19 May 1978.
14. *Ag*, the newsletter of Compassion in World Farming, January 1980.
15. 'Information on behaviour and diseases of the laying hen', presented by the Society for Veterinary Ethology to the Standing Committee of the European Convention for the Protection of Animals Kept for Farming Purposes, 25 April 1980. All information in this paragraph is taken from this report.
16. '£10 Chick Levy', *Poultry World*, 14 October 1982.

17. 'Eggs Dear if Batteries Axed' *Yorkshire Post*, 12 April 1980.
18. R. Harrison, *Animal Machines*, Stuart Publications 1964.
19. Ministry of Agriculture statistics, 1980/1.
20. 'Case for the mini-mother', *World Poultry Industry*, October 1981.
21. 'Standing room only at leg session', *Poultry World*, 12 November 1981.
22. 'Broiler growth rates suffer as latest disease hazard strikes', *Poultry World*, 15 October 1981.
23. Ministry of Agriculture statistics.
24. *Ibid*.
25. Ministry of Agriculture, *Codes of Recommendations for the Welfare of Livestock and Domestic Fowls*, (Code no.3) August 1971.
26. Ministry of Agriculture statistics.
27. Figures based upon practices at Bernard Matthews Ltd, Great Witchingham, near Norwich, Norfolk.
28. Article on Webb and Webb Poultry Processors, Bradford, *Poultry World*, 4 March 1982.
29. Ministry of Agriculture, *Slaughter of Poultry (Humane Conditions) Regulations 1971*, HMSO 1971.
30. Farm Animal Welfare Council, *The Welfare of Poultry at the Time of Slaughter*, HMSO January 1982.
31. *Ibid*.
32. Letter signed by Peter Walker, Minister of Agriculture, to Richard Needham MP concerning conditions at a poultry processing plant at Sutton Benger, Wiltshire, 30 July 1980.
33. Farm Animal Welfare Council, *The Welfare of Poultry at the Time of Slaughter*.
34. 'BFP wants to double up on old hen time', *Poultry World*, 20 May 1982.

## 2. Pigs and cattle

1. Percentages estimated from Ministry of Agriculture statistics.
2. Ministry of Agriculture figures quoted in *Daily Mail*, 15 October 1970.
3. 'Who does what in pig production', *British Farmer and Stockbreeder*, 5 July 1980.
4. 'Semen with Staying Power', *Farming News*, 15 April 1983.
5. *Pigs-Service Management*, Ministry of Agriculture's Advisory and Development Department (ADAS) 1979.
6. Fred Anderson, Unit Manager, Glebe plantation piggeries, speaking

in *Pig Farming*, March 1983.

7. 'Welfare and the sow stall', *Pig Farming*, October 1981.

8. For example, Professor John Webster on BBC documentary 'Down on the Factory Farm', June 1979.

9. N. Hicks, *Fishwick's Pigs. Their Breeding, Feeding and Management* , 8th ed. Crosby Lockwood, 1961.

10. House of Commons Select Committee on Agriculture, *Report on Animal Welfare in Poultry, Pig and Veal Calf Production*, 1981, para. 116.

11. Farm Animal Welfare Council, *Revised Codes of Recommendations for the Welfare of Pigs*, Ministry of Agriculture, March 1980.

12. 'One little pig went to market − but too many of his brothers were ill at home', *British Farmer and Stockbreeder*, 15 August 1981.

13. *Ibid*.

14. *Ibid*.

15. 'Whitehall is warned on pig disease', *East Anglian Daily Times*, 7 November 1981.

16. D.W. Forsyth, 'Atypical oedema disease', *Pig Veterinary Society Proceedings*, vol.6, 1980.

17. M.R. Muirhead, 'Porcine pneumonia. Its differential diagnosis and the control of mycoplasma hyopneumonia', *Pig Veterinary Society Proceedings*, vol.6, 1980.

18. *Ibid*.

19. D. Sainsbury, 'Getting to grips with growth promoters', *Pig Farming*, January 1982.

20. 'An ounce of prevention', Ministry of Agriculture film, 1981.

21. A.B. Kovacs and G.M. Beer, 'The mechanical properties and qualities of floors for pigs in relation to limb disorders', *Pig Veterinary Proceedings*, vol.5, 1979.

22. H.D. Pattison, 'Patterns of sow culling', *Pig News and Information*, vol.1, no.3, 1980.

23. 'Minutes of Evidence from UK agricultural departments to House of Commons Select Committee on Animal Welfare', HMSO, 1981 p.57.

24. *Ibid*. In fact in evidence to the committee the Agriculture Department 'estimated that up to 40 per cent of veal is produced using loose housing in small groups', leaving the other 60 per cent in crates.

25. Ministry of Agriculture census, December 1981.

26. O. King, 'Husbandry methods predisposing to production disease in dairy cows', *Veterinary Record*, 27 June 1981.

27. Figure quoted from 'The Animals Film' directed by Victor Schonfeld, Slick Pics Ltd, London, 1981.

## 3. To the slaughter

1. A.W. Carter, 'Markets', talk from the Livestock and Market Commission at the Humane Treatment of Food Animals in Transit Symposium organized by the University Federation for Animal Welfare, Potters Bar: UFAW 1979.
2. 'Dealers' calves are banned from market', *Farmers' Weekly*, 30 April 1982.
3. The *News of the World* team accompanied Mrs Eileen Bizet of the Dartmoor Livestock Protection Society on the journey. Mrs Bizet's account can be read in the June quarterly of the Raystede Centre for Animal Welfare, Ringmer, East Sussex.
4. Statement from the Ministry of Agriculture, 16 August 1978.
5. 'Our exports could ruin us say farmers', *Shropshire Star*, 26 July 1982.
6. A.W. Carter, 'Markets'. Talk given at the Humane Treatment of Food Animals in Transit Symposium.
7. The Ammedown Group, 'report of a seminar on the transport and slaughter of animals', 16 – 18 April 1980, Council of Justice for Animals and Humane Slaughter Association, Potters Bar.
8. 'Poor transport causing pig carcase damage', *Scottish Farmer*, 11 December 1982.
9. *Ibid*.
10. A.G. Sains 'Transport' talk from the Humane Treatment of Food Animals in Transit Symposium, University Federation for Animal Welfare, 1979.
11. *Ibid*.
12. *The Slaughtering Industry in Great Britain 1980 – 81*, Meat and Livestock Industry 1982. All slaughterhouse figures are measured in cattle units, rather than total number of animals killed.
13. Some Muslim leaders, like the Imam of Woking, actively support pre-stunning of animals, and some ritual slaughterhouses (e.g. Slough) carry out stunning for Muslim-consumed meat.
14. The Ammedown Group, report of a seminar.
15. Written evidence presented by David Whiting to the Farm Animal Welfare Council, 20 November 1981.
16. The captive bolt pistol is placed on the animal's forehead and when 'fired' lets out a long bolt into the brain and out again.

17. A. Mews, 'Do abattoirs need to change their ways?' *Meat Magazine*, September 1981.
18. 'Recent developments in Dutch slaughter line', *Meat Magazine*, March 1980.
19. 'High-voltage stunning need not impair bleeding-out', *Meat Magazine*, July 1981.
20. J. Gracey, 'Animal welfare is the key to higher quality meat' *Meat Magazine*, November 1981.
21. 'Memoirs of a slaughterman', an unpublished paper presented to Compassion in World Farming by Burnbake Art Exhibition for Prison Artists, 56 Welbeck Avenue, Southampton.

## 4. Enter the health hazards

1. The Association of the British Pharmaceutical Industry, *Annual Report 1980 − 81*.
2. *Ibid*.
3. D. Sainsbury, 'Getting to grips with growth promoters', *Pig Farming*, January 1982.
4. 'Not pure science fiction', *Veterinary Record*, 9 June 1979.
5. 'Antibiotic resistance. Where does the blame lie?' *Veterinary Record*, 27 September 1980.
6. M.R. Muirhead, 'Porcine pneumonia. Its differential diagnosis and the control of mycoplasma hyopneumonia', *Pig Veterinary Society Proceedings*, vol.6, 1980.
7. Quoted in 'Salmonellosis', *Ag*, the newsletter of Compassion in World Farming, no.60, September 1980.
8. 'Salmonellosis in animals and man', *Veterinary Record*, 14 November 1981.
9. *Ibid*.
10. *Ibid*.
11. *Ibid*.
12. 'Salmonellosis: a continuing problem', *Veterinary Record*, 14 November 1981.
13. 'Salmonellosis in animals and man', *Veterinary Record*, 14 November 1981.
14. A. Tucker, 'Back to germ welfare', first printed in *The Guardian*, 1980, reprinted in *Ag*, no.60, September 1980.
15. *Ibid*.
16. *Ibid*.
17. R. Norton-Taylor, 'BBC in row over animal drugs hazard, *The*

*Guardian*, 8 May 1979.

18. N. Tyler, 'The "superbug" danger in the meat we eat', *Now!*, 28 November 1980.

19. 'What price your vet's survival', *British Farmer and Stockbreeder*, 20 March 1982.

20. 'Animal medicine and the EEC', *Veterinary Record*, 6 November 1982.

21. 'Growth promoters: threat of ban recedes at last', *British Farmer and Stockbreeder*, 7 February 1981.

22. *Ibid*.

23. H. Clayton, 'Loopholes in drug laws', *The Times*, 13 May 1981.

24. M. Hornsby, 'EEC backs down on hormone ban', *The Times*, 13 May 1981.

25. *Ibid*.

26. *Pig Farming*, January 1983, p.19.

27. 'Winning at chemical roulette', *British Farmer and Stockbreeder*, 8 September 1979.

28. M. Winstanley, 'Concern over abattoir hygiene', *Meat Magazine*, July 1980.

29. *Ibid*.

30. 'Lower levels of nitrite and nitrate are recommended', *Meat Traders' Journal*, 4 January 1979.

31. 'Polyphosphates and water uptake', *Poultry Industry*, 1 July 1980.

## 5. Human violence and animal suffering

1. D.H. Lawrence, 'Aristocracy' *Phoenix 11*, Heinemann, 1968.

2. *Farmer and Stockbreeder*, 30 Janurary 1962. Quoted from J. Mason and P. Singer, *Animal Factories*, Crown Publishers, New York: 1980.

3. J. Seymour, *Bring Me My Bow*, Turnstone Books 1977, pp.145-47. Reprinted by kind permission of the publisher.

4. G.A.H. Wells, 'Genetical, physiological and anatomical factors in baby pigs contributing to foot and limb disorders and other injuries attributed to floors', *Pig Veterinary Society Proceedings*, vol.4, 1979.

5. G. van Putten and J. Dammerj, 'A comparative study of the well-being of piglets reared conventionally and in cages', *Applied Animal Ethology*, vol.2, Amsterdam: Elsevier 1976, pp. 339-56.

6. 'How Sir John's chickens came home to roost', *Daily Mail*, 12 September 1978.

7. E.F. Schumacher, *Small is Beautiful*, Abacus 1974, p.88.
8. *The Guardian*, 8 January 1983.
9. 'Run by amateurs', *Meat Magazine*, July 1982.
10. In the UK both the Rowett Research Institute and the Grassland Institute have undertaken research on this.
11. 'Broiler growth rate rise to continue', *Meat Traders' Journal*, 21 February 1980.
12. *Cotswold Progress*, the newsletter of the Cotswold Pig Development Co. Ltd, no 13, Autumn 1982.
13. *Ibid*.
14. *Ag*, the newsletter of Compassion in World Farming, January 1980.
15. The *Daily Star* ran a series of articles, with photographs, on Babraham, June to September 1979.
16. 'Weaned into waste bins' *Pig Farming*, August 1980.

## 6. Myth one: scientific objectivity

1. 'We need fact − not emotion', *Farmers' Guardian*, 4 May 1979.
2. *Ibid*.
3. *Ibid*.
4. *Sense or Sentiment*, National Farmers' Union, 1980.
5. 'Emotion versus reason', *Farmers' Weekly*, 9 October 1981.
6. Letter from the Ministry of Agriculture to Compassion in World Farming, 29 June 1978.
7. Sir R. Butler, opening address at the Humane Treatment of Animals in Transit Symposium organized by University Federation for Animal Welfare, Potters Bar: UFAW 1979.
8. FAWAC, *The Welfare of Livestock*, HMSO 1970.
9. *Ibid*.
10. M. Stamp-Dawkins, *Animal Suffering*, Chapman & Hall 1980, pp. 88 − 89.
11. 'Answer the welfarists with facts', *Farmers' Guardian*, 1980, quoted in *Ag*, the newsletter of Compassion in World farming, no. 59, June 1980.
12. 'Raise sheep like hogs', *US Farm Journal*, November 1979.
13. *Ibid*.
14. Sir K. Blaxter, Response to criticism of rearing piglets at birth, Rowett Research Institute, October 1980.
15. *Ag*, no. 54, June/July 1979.
16. B. Roach, 'Agro at feeding time', *Pig Farming*, October 1981.
17. E.F. Schumacher, *Small is Beautiful*, Abacus 1974, p.66.

18. H.A. Elson, 'No conclusive evidence on need to change production systems', *Poultry Forum*, March 1980.
19. G. van Putten, 'Ever been close to a nosey pig?' *Applied Animal Ethology*, vol.5, 1979, p.298.
20. G. van Putten, 'Comfort behaviour in pigs and its significance regarding their well-being', European Association for Animal Production 28th Meeting, Brussels, 25 August 1977.
21. *Ibid.*
22. R. Ingrams (ed.), *Cobbett's Country Book*, Schochen 1975.
23. W. Cobbett, *Journal of a Year's Residence In America*, Centaur Press 1964.

## 7. Myth two: public demand

1. Statistics estimated by the Vegetarian Society (UK).
2. 'More competition for the 'free' compound trade', *Poultry World*, 19 November 1981.
3. *Ibid.*
4. Goldenlay Eggs UK are the largest marketing consortium for eggs in the country.
5. 'More competition for the 'free' compound trade', *Poultry World*, 19 November 1981.
6. *Ibid.*
7. R. Norton-Taylor, *Whose Land is it Anyway?*, Turnstone Press 1982, p.117.
8. Ministry of Agriculture slaughtering statistics.
9. Figures established from information supplied by *Quarterly Digest of Advertising Expenditure*, Media Expenditure Analysis Ltd (MEAL) September 1981.
10. 'FT use tv power', *Meat Magazine*, December 1981.
11. 'A fitting return', *Meat Traders' Journal*, February 1982.
12. *Ibid.*
13. C. Wardle, *Changing Food Habits in The UK*, Earth Resources Ltd 1977.
14. 'Poultrymeat number one', *Poultry World*, 11 February 1982.
15. C. Tudge, *The Famine Business*, Pelican 1977, p.66.
16. 'Yet More Takeovers', *Poultry Industry*, 1 November 1979.
17. 'More competition for the 'free' compound trade', *Poultry World*, 19 November 1981.
18. 'Yet More Takeovers', *Poultry Industry*, 1 November 1979.
19. R. Pasmore *el al.* 'Prescription for a better diet', *British Medical*

*Journal*, vol.52, no.7, 1979.

20. 'If you're overweight, try eating more bread and potatoes', Health Education Council Advertisement in *Daily Mirror*, 28 February 1983.

21. 'Tinkering with or retooling the NHS is not what is needed', the Reith Lectures 1980, no.3, reprinted in *The Listener*, 20 November 1980.

22. J. Mason and P. Singer, *Animal Factories*, New York: Crown Publishers 1980.

## 8. Myth three: the solution to world hunger

1. 'Extensive systems up egg costs by 20p a doz', *Poultry World*, 1 March 1979.

2. P. Roberts, 'Put humans first', *Ag*, the newsletter of Compassion in World Farming, no.65, December 1981.

3. J. Mason and P. Singer, *Animal Factories*, New York: Crown Publishers 1980, p.74.

4. F. Moore Lappe, *Diet for a Small Planet*, New York: Ballantine Books 1971, p.10.

5. P. Harrison, 'The inequalities that curb potential', *Ceres*, no. 81, vol.14, no.3, May/June 1981; figures taken originally from the Food and Agricultural Organization.

6. G. Leech, *Energy and Food Production*, IPC Science and Technology Press 1976.

7. *Output and Utilization of Farm Produce in the UK, 1974 − 80*, Government Statistical Services.

8. C. Tudge, *The Famine Business*, Pelican 1977.

9. 'Agricultural production efficiency', *New York Times*, 13 January 1975.

10. The Politics of Health Group, *Food and Profit*, pamphlet no.1, c/o British Society for Social Responsibility in Science, 1980.

11. Import figures 1979 − 81 obtained from HM Customs and Excise, Statistical Department, Southend.

12. *Output and Utilization of Farm Produce in the UK, 1974 − 80*, Government Statistical Services.

13. 'The hungry and the fed', leaflet issued by Compassion In World Farming, based on work with the Central Food Technology Research Institute, Mysore, India.

14. R. Norton-Taylor, *Whose Land is it Anyway?* Turnstone Books 1982, p.311.

15. The Politics of Health Group, *Food and Profit*.
16. D. Scott, 'Hunger in the Eighties', *Ceres* no.81, vol.14, no.3, May/June 1981.
17.  P. Harrison, 'The inequalities that curb potential'.
18. For further discussion of USA manipulation of agriculture in Latin America, see F. Moor Lappe, *Diet for a Small Planet*.
19. 'An opportunity that must be grasped. Peter Walker lays foundation for trade boost with Brazil and Argentina', Ministry of Agriculture press notice, 23 September 1981.
20. 'Lord Ferrers completes tour of agriculture in Middle East Countries', Ministry of Agriculture press notice, 18 September 1981.
21. *Bangladesh Information Sheet*, Oxfam Information Service, 29 September 1977.
22. 'Cages for Bangladesh', *Poultry World*, 1 February 1979.
23. *Whitaker's Almanac*, 1979.
24. *Bangladesh Information Sheet*, Oxfam.
25. J.K. Boyce and B. Hartmann, 'Hunger in a fertile land', *Ceres*, March/April 1981.
26. 'India's booming poultry industry', *Poultry Industry*, February 1980.
27. '*Ibid*.
28. 'Malaysia reaches self-sufficiency in poultry meat', *Poultry Industry*, October 1981.
29. *Ibid*.
30. Information supplied by HM Customs and Excise, Statistical Department, Southend.
31. C. Tudge, *The Famine Business*, p.69.

## 9. Myth four: happy workers

1. S. Mansholt, *The Common Agricultural Policy. Some New Thinking*, The Soil Association, Walnut Tree Manor, Haughley, Suffolk, 1979.
2. C. Tudge, *The Famine Business*, Pelican 1977.
3. 'Farmer falls foul of chicken check rules', *Daily Telegraph*, 22 January 1982.
4. 'Economics and treatment − the vet's dilemma' *Farmers' Weekly*, 9 October 1982.
5. 'Cages best for owners, workers, consumers and birds', *Poultry World*, 10 April 1980.
6. 'House of Commons Debate on European Community Proposals

(Battery Hens)', *Hansard*, HMSO, 17 November 1981.
7. 'Pigs in the open air', *Farmers' Weekly*, 21 November 1980.
8. 'When people are happy so are the pigs', *Farmers' Weekly*, 18 April 1980.
9. 'Pigs in the open air', *Farmers' Weekly*.
10. E.F. Schumacher, *Small is Beautiful*, Abacus, 1974.
11. 'Is there life at the end of the contract', *Poultry World*, 26 June 1980.
12. 'The human cost', *Ag*, no.59, June 1980.
13. 'Health record stinks', *Farmers' Weekly*, 9 November 1979.
14. *Ibid*.
15. *Ibid*.

## 10. Myth five: economic necessity

1. E.F. Schumacher, *Small is Beautiful*, Abacus 1974, p.34.
2. *The Protection of Birds Act, 1954*, HMSO.
3. Wording originates from *The Protection of Animals Act, 1911*, HMSO.
4. Statement made by David Barker, NFU Suffolk Branch at National Farmers' Union AGM, 9 February 1982.
5. M. Shoard, *The Theft of the Countryside*, Maurice Temple-Smith 1980, p.29.
6. Royal Commission on Environmental Pollution, *Agriculture and Pollution*, seventh report, HMSO 1979, p.128, para. 6.
7. *Ibid*. p.130 para. 10.
8. *Ibid*. p.134 para. 23.
9. *Ibid*. p.131 para. 14.
10. *Ibid*. p.132 para. 14.
11. *Ibid*. p.138 para. 31.
12. House of Commons Select Committee on Agriculture, *Report on Animal Welfare in Poultry, Pigs and Veal Calf Production*, HMSO 1981, (Tax Reliefs for Intensive Farming, Appendix 5 Para. 6.)
13. *Ibid*. para. 7.
14. *Ibid*. para. 2.
15. Figures supplied by EEC Office, Intervention Department, Reading, UK.
16. 'No easy answer to surplus grain', *British Farmer and Stockbreeder*, 20 March 1982.
17. B. Wilson, 'The only good cow is a dead cow', *New Statesman*, 29 February 1980.

18. Figures supplied by EEC Office, Intervention Department, Reading, UK.
19. *Ibid*.
20. *Poultry World*, 7 January 1982.
21. The Worcestershire NFU, *Record for farmers and growers*, vol.55, no.14, 1979.
22. 'Fast Food openings for egg products', *Farmers' Guardian*, 25 September 1981.
23. *Output and Utilization of Farm Produce in the UK*, Government Statistical Services.
24. Investigation undertaken by UK Egg Producers Association, August 1980.
25. '1982 meat sales rise by £100 million', *Poultry World*, 3 March 1983.
26. 'Welfare groups go to work on eggs', *Farmers' Weekly*, 31 October 1980.
27. M. Pitt, 'Report of a visit to France, Denmark, Germany, Holland and Switzerland to study the production and marketing of non-cage eggs', Nuffield Farming Scholarship Trust Award, 1982.
28. 'Countdown to a cageless society', *Poultry World*, 30 September 1982.
29. Ministry of Agriculture, *Annual Review of Agriculture 1982*, HMSO.
30. A point first noted by Chickens' Lib, 6 Pilling Lane, Skelman-thorpe, Huddersfield, West Yorkshire.
31. S. Mansholt, *The Common Agricultural Policy. Some New Thinking*, The Soil Association, New Bells Farm, Haughley, Stowmarket, Suffolk.
32. M. Shoard, *The Theft of the Countryside*.
33. *Ibid*.
34. '£53.8 million cleans egg off Imperial's poultry face', *Poultry World*, 8 April 1982.
35. *Ibid*.
36. *Ibid*.
37. *Ibid*.
38. *Ibid*.
39. *Cotswold Progress*, newsletter of the Cotswold Pig Development Co. Ltd, no.13, Autumn 1982.
40. J. Conrad, *Chance*, Methuen, first published 1914.
41. *Ibid*.

## 11. Alternatives

1. 'Calf rearing', *Farmers' Weekly*, 5 March 1971.
2. *Veterinary Record*, 31 May 1980; figures quoted were £175 per calf in crates and £78 per calf in loose-housing system.
3. 'Calf rearing', *Farmers' Weekly*.
4. For example, see 'Success with deep-litter', *Poultry Farmer, May 1980*.
5. *'The straw-yard system'*, *Ag*, the newsletter of Compassion in World Farming, no. 52, January 1979.
6. 'Report on first year of Ministry of Agriculture research into aviary system', *Poultry World*, 18 November 1982.
7. Martin Pitt produces eggs for many retail outlets from his aviary system at Levatt's Farm, Clench Common, Nr Marlborough, Wiltshire.
8. For details of the Getaway cage, see 'Cages of the future', *Farmers' Guardian*, 29 March 1974.
9. House of Commons Select Committee on Agriculture, *Report on animal welfare in poultry, pigs and veal calf production*, session 1980-81, HMSO, para. 144.
10. M. Pitt 'Report of a visit to France, Denmark, Germany, Holland and Switzerland to study the production and marketing of non-cage eggs', Nuffield Farming Scholarship Award, 1982.
11. *Ibid*.
12. *New facts. 3D System Makes Room for Laying Hens*, Aktie Lekker Dier, Jansweld 45, 35 12 B6 Utrecht, Holland, November 1981, p.7.
13. For example, Mr Derek Jewell, who keeps over 20,000 hens on deep-litter at Gardeners Farm, Nr Romsey, Hants.
14. Ministry of Agriculture's Advisory Department (ADAS), 'A cost comparison of commercial egg production', Farm Animal Welfare Group, 1981.
15. Lecture in May 1981 at Celle, West Germany, reported in *New Facts. 3D System Makes Room for Laying Hens*.
16. House of Commons Select Committee on Agriculture, *Report on animal welfare in poultry, pigs and veal calf production*, para. 137.
17. P. Carnell, 'An economic appraisal of less intensive systems', in *Alternatives To Intensive Husbandry Systems*, University Federation for Animal Welfare, 1981.
18. *Ibid*.
19. *Ibid*.

20. *Ibid.*
21. For instance, Fermier Landias — Marie Hot, a co-operative of more than 300 farmers in south-west France.
22. 'Slower growth rates to cut leg problems', *Poultry World*, 14 January 1982.
23. 'Houses where air is free', *Poultry World*, 1 June 1980.
24. *Ibid.*
25. *Ibid.*
26. *Ibid.*
27. M. Boddington, *Outdoor Pig Production. Report on an Economic Investigation*, Wye College, University of London, Ashford, Kent, 1971.
28. 'Come-back for outdoor pig keeping', *Pig Farming*, July 1981.
29. *Ibid.*
30. *Ibid.*
31. 'Crate farrowing comes under suspicion', *Farmers' Weekly*, pig production extra, 11 July 1980.
32. 'Five-week Weaning', *Farmers' Weekly*, 26 March 1982.
33. *Revised Code of Recommendations for the Welfare of Pigs, (Draft)*, March 1980. Farm Animal Welfare Council. MAFF Government Buildings, Hook Rise South, Tolworth, Surrey.
34. 'Happy families — the secret of profitable pig farming', *Farmers' Weekly*, 13 March 1981.
35. 'New hope for orphan lambs', *The Times*, 24 November 1981.
36. 'Lambs saved from the cold', *Farmers' Weekly*, 22 January 1982.

## 12. Small is preferable

1. 'Eggs in grain and manioc fight', *Poultry World*, 18 February 1982.
2. 'Government gives welfare council a voice in research', *Poultry World*, 10 June 1982.
3. 'The composition and nutritive value of white lupin', *Nutrition Abstracts and Reviews*, Series B, vol.47, no.8, 1977, p.523.
4. *Ibid.* p.522.
5. *Ibid.* p.523.
6. 'Government cuts mean end of work on oats', *Scottish Farmer*, 4 August 1979.
7. See for example 'Kept in the dark', a film about farm animals for children, produced by Compassion in World Farming, Petersfield, Hants, 1981.
8. 'Why farmers need chemicals', *Shell Education News*, no.10,

Summer 1982.

9. G. Leech, *Energy and Food Production*, IPC Science and Technology Press, 1976.

10. R. Norton-Taylor, *Whose Land is it Anyway?*, Turnstone Press 1982, p.199.

11. S. Mansholt, *The Common Agricultural Policy. Some new thinking*, The Soil Association, 1979.

12. *Ibid*.

## 13. Taking action

1. D. Jee, 'Time to counter welfare claptrap', *Poultry World*, 20 August 1981.

# Useful addresses and books

### Anti-factory farming

*Compassion in World Farming*, 20 Lavant Street, Petersfield, Hants GU32 3EW. The most active national society campaigning against factory farming, with a network of local groups around the country. Organizes demonstrations, produces newsletter, campaign leaflets, educational kits and films.

*The Farm and Food Society*, 4 Willifield Way, London NW11 7XT. Less of a 'demonstrating' organization than CIWF, but produces informative literature.

*Chickens' Lib*, 6 Pilling Lane, Skelmanthorpe, Huddersfield, West Yorks. A small, enthusiastic and active group dedicated to the abolition of the battery cage for laying hens.

*Animal Aid*, 111 High Street, Tonbridge, Kent. Although primarily an anti-vivisection society, this particularly active group sees its role as to fight all animal abuse. Increasingly, this has involved excursions into fighting factory farming with the 'meat means misery' campaign. Its large network of local groups produces informative literature (including a newsletter), educational films and filmstrips.

### Pro-factory farming

*The National Farmers' Union*, Agriculture House, Knightsbridge, London SW1X 7NJ. The powerful NFU will, no doubt, be delighted to try to discount all the arguments put forward in this book. They have produced booklets, films and leaflets in an attempt to defend factory farming.

## Food reform

*The Vegan Society*, 47 Highlands Road, Leatherhead, Surrey. The rapidly expanding society which promotes a diet free from all animal produce on moral, health, ecological and economic grounds. Produces excellent literature on all aspects.

*The Vegetarian Society (UK)*, 53, Marloes Road, London W8 6LA Branches around the country. Promotes vegetarianism through its magazine, cookery demonstrations, leaflets, etc. Also excellent annual handbook, with guides to vegatarian hotels, restaurants, etc.

## Organic farming

*The Soil Association*, Walnut Tree Manor, Haughley, Stowmarket, Suffolk. Promotes the theory and practice of organic farming. Courses, groups and excellent literature. For gardeners too.

*Henry Doubleday Association*, Bocking, Braintree, Essex. As above.

## Direct action

*Animal Liberation Front*, PO Box 190, 8 Elm Avenue, Nottingham. For those who believe that 'stealing' animals from factory farms and laboratories and damage to property is both justified and necessary to the campaign for animal rights.

## Youth groups

*Youth For Animal Rights*, Hillview, Chaffcombe, Nr Chard TA20 4AH. Promotes the cause of animal rights, particularly, though not exclusively laboratory and farm animals with young people of school age. The official young persons' branch of Compassion in World Farming and one of the country's most active anti-vivisection societies, Animal Aid, 111 High Street, Tonbridge, Kent.

## Cookery books

*The Bean Book*. Rose Elliot. Fontana, 1979. Perhaps the best of many books by the same author featuring mostly lacto-vegetarian recipes.

*Vegan Cooking: The Compassionate Way of Eating*. Leah Leneman. Thorsons, 1982. The most recent vegan cookbook, featuring many interesting recipes.

*What's Cooking*. Eva Batt. The Vegan Society, 1980. Written by one of the pioneers of the vegan movement, this book contains excellent advice on nutrition, as well as a full choice of meals.

*The Good Housekeeping Book of Wholefood Cookery*. Gail Duff. Ebury Press, 1980. There are now a whole range of good lacto-vegetarian cookery books. The particular strength of this one is the excellent information on the principles of wholefood cookery.

Charlie Clutterbuck and Tim Lang
**More than we can chew**
The crazy world of food and farming

'it brings us face to face, in chapter after chapter, with aspects of the grisly politics of food. It should be read by everyone who earns their living by producing food... it should probably be read by the rest of us too' *The Landworker*

'helps to illuminate the absurdity of the international agricultural trading system' *The Guardian*

'excellent study of Europe and particularly the Common Agricultural Policy of the EEC' *Morning Star*

£2.50      paperback      ISBN 0 86104 501 7

Philip Windeatt
# The Hunt and the Anti-Hunt

'Phil Windeatt's concise and pointed account of the battle over bloodsports is an important booklet which covers much new ground, summarising as it does the history of hunting and anti-hunting legislation together with details of hunt sab tactics — all couched in a wider political and social context... More power to his pen.' *Undercurrents*

'a handbook that is well written and concise... Books are weapons — arm yourself with this one and come out fighting.' *The Liberator*

£1.95        paperback        ISBN 0 86104 387 1

Pluto books are available through your local bookshop. In case of difficulty contact Pluto to find out local stocklists or to obtain catalogues/leaflets. If all else fails write to:

**Pluto Press Limited**
**Freepost**, (no stamp required)
**105A, Torriano Avenue**
**London NW5 1YP**

To order, enclose a cheque/p.o. payable to Pluto Press to cover price of book, plus 50p per book for postage and packing (£2.50 maximum). Telephone 01-482 1973.